Things said about .

By people

"Absolutely tore through it. Brilliantly written."
Pete Astor

"...your very entertaining book."
John Niven

"This is so moving!! I loved it... One way or another this will be a beautiful thing in the world."
Sukie Smith

"It's very funny and [a] literally revelatory story of his life and times with the Rockingbirds, before and since. You're going to love it."
Sean Read

And by a few who aren't...

"Alan Tyler proves just as good a story-teller over book length as song length."
Andrew Mueller

"A funny, moving and above all unique memoir from the most talented musician you only think you've heard of.
It's a great book."
David Quantick

"It is absolutely bloody marvellous."
John Mitchinson

ALAN TYLER

HOW TO NEVER HAVE A HIT

The confessions of an unsuccessful singer-songwriter

First published in 2025

Copyright © Alan Tyler 2025

All rights reserved.
No part of this publication may be reproduced in any form or by any means without the written permission of the publisher.

ISBN: 978-1-0685345-2-2

www.alantyler.com

For Alyson, my sister

CONTENTS

	Foreword by John Niven	9
	Prologue	13
1.	The D'Arcy Drive Sound	19
2.	Swing Gently	46
3.	A Brief Prehistory Of The Rockingbirds	70
4.	Cowboys In Camden Town	91
5.	Agoristo	114
6.	The Blue Man	136
7.	In Tall Buildings	151
8.	Spirit Of The West	172
9.	Rockingbirds Reunited	185
10.	Yesterday's Chips	212
	Discography	242
	Picture information	244
	Acknowledgements	246

Foreword
by John Niven

THERE CAN BE a lot in a single glance. Some glances you will spend a lifetime unpacking.

The late summer of 1992. We're in Aberdeen, in the bar of a decent hotel. A Marriott or Holiday Inn type deal. The night before, The Rockingbirds blew Glasgow's King Tut's Wah Wah Hut apart. Encore after encore. Sweat pouring off the low ceiling onto the crowd. It is a little after 7am the following morning and we – a group of musicians, road crew and hangers-on – are playing poker. Very clearly, we have not troubled our beds. Along with the morning sun, a group of businessmen are beginning to filter through the bar on their way to breakfast. They are besuited, and we too are in our uniforms: road worn denim and cowboy boots and five-day stubble. As they pass a couple of them look over at us – and at the bottles, the cards, the overflowing ashtrays – with undisguised contempt, their stares saying something like *'ow on earth did you bums come to be staying in a hotel like this?'* The singer glances up from his fanned cards and meets their gaze. Over the last 30 years I have thought a lot about how he met the gaze of those businessmen. In a novel he would be described as meeting it 'evenly'. Better yet to say he returned those stares with added topspin. For the singer's eyes were saying...

> *'I am living the life I have dreamed of since I was a kid. I am not going to have to cram a full English breakfast into myself at the crack of dawn before hurrying off to spend the day sweating into a cheap shirt in a miserable conference room. I have been up all night laughing and drinking and dancing and playing music and roaring my way through my time and I will soon retire to bed to sleep until the early afternoon, when I will rise and climb aboard the tour bus and head down the highway to another town where I will do it all over again and I will never have to shave off my hair and go to work in tall buildings and it will be glorious.'*

Of course, as you'll learn in these pages, it didn't quite work out like that for Alan Tyler. Like most of us, he did eventually have to trim his hair and go to work in tall buildings. But, along the way, from writing *Jonathan Jonathan* as the eighties ended right through to writing *Deptford Creek* as the twenties began, there were always the songs. Thirty years of brilliant songs without a hit record beyond a solitary novelty cover version. How on earth do you manage that?

Read on, my friend, read on...

I WAS TRAVELLING to work one morning on the Bakerloo line, in the no-man's land between South Kenton station and North Wembley, when my moment of epiphany occurred. Planning an event to mark the 100th anniversary of the birth of Hank Williams (born on the 17th of September 1923) I was immersing myself in all the great country singer had done by listening through the 225 recordings of *The Complete Hank Williams*. As I listened, my random play arrived at *How To Write Folk And Western Music To Sell*. Referring not to a song but to a book, this recorded curiosity is taken from an old radio show, with the presenter conducting a scripted conversation with the Hillbilly Shakespeare to advertise the singing star's new book, priced at one dollar. Hank explained:

"Friends I have had thousands and thousands and thousands of letters from you folks who have written in to me and asked

me how you can go about getting a song published, or how you can get an artist to record your song. So I decided that somebody ought to give all these people some help, for who knows, there may be a great song out there somewhere in somebody's dresser drawer just waiting to be sung..."

Amused and inspired by this, I was struck by an idea: if old Hank could do business sharing the secret of his songwriting success for a dollar a time, perhaps I, a songwriter who has never written a hit, could share the secret of his failure in a book sold for considerably more?

Though flaws in this reasoning may be evident, its perverseness appealed to me. If I am never to be a remarkable success in music, perhaps I might still make my name in print as a notable failure at it. Doesn't Tolstoy's famous maxim, that "all happy families are alike, but every unhappy family is unhappy in its own way", affirm that failure is so much more interesting than success?

Of course, as was so with Hank Williams, we all know that fame and success are not necessarily bringers of joy and contentment. However, it should also be noted that this is a truism put about mainly by those who prevail, to the point where we may completely overlook that a lack of fame and fortune can also be a considerable bummer. History is written by the victors, we are told; well, not this time. "Write about what you know" is what they also say. Well, failure is what I do know... so here goes.

When it comes to writing, I am an avowed Platonist. Good writing, like all good art, is not a meaning made, it is a truth discovered and revealed. The idea of Hank's book was the clue that gave me the key to discovering my own, and the torrent of recollections and reflections that issued from my teeming brain once the idea had taken hold in me made me sure that the book was, in a real sense, already there, and a necessary thing. All I had to do was to hold out my cowboy hat to catch the coins tumbling from the fruit machine of my mojo.

So I accept not much credit nor blame for this thing which I now bring you. I am but the medium and the messenger. The writing of the book is just something that had to be done, whatever the consequences (or lack of them) may prove to be.

At this point, I will admit an objection to this whole conceit, which is that I am not the great failure I claim to be, that I exaggerate my case, and that the premise for my book is therefore invalid.

It is true that I have had some good friends and supporters who have thought well of what I and my musical compañeros have done, and I am most grateful for any praise and encouragement that has thus come my way. Some of those kind givers include people of standing in the music industry, which has meant a number of records have been made and released, songs published, and engagements received and performed, over a period of four decades and more.

But though my admirers may say I have, in fact, done very well, this sentiment is not reflected in the data. The first Rockingbirds album, my first release of note, which had a significant section of the UK music press rooting for it, sold, I believe, around 12,000 copies. 12,000 is a level of sales I would love to repeat now, but for a major label release in 1992 (or in any other year) it was far from being a success. After we were dropped by Sony, The Rockingbirds' follow-up album on Cooking Vinyl/Heavenly sold half that of the first, and then my first solo album in 2001 stretched only to a pressing of 2000. Since then, pressings have gone down from 1000 CD runs to 500 a time for the last couple of releases. My dear friends at Hanky Panky Records have not told me how many copies my last album, *Made In Middlesex,* has sold, and I have not asked them. I *never* ask.

As to present day online metrics, by which one's popularity is now recorded with such excruciating accuracy, Spotify analytics tell me The Rockingbirds muster around 300 monthly listeners, and my various solo incarnations usually clock up less than 100 listeners a month. Most of these listeners, the website further informs me, are male and over 50 (and God bless them, every one).

It is true I have been on *Top Of The Pops*, which is (or was) a widely-accepted marker of "making it'. I was fronting The Rockingbirds, performing a song from a record that reached No. 26 in the singles chart in November, 1992. But Heavenly's *Fred EP* was credited in the chart rundown not to The Rockingbirds but to "Various" (the other contributors to this Terrence Higgins Trust charity effort being Saint Etienne and Flowered Up). In short, it was not our record. Some will say that this is nitpicking, and it does not matter; we had a hit, and I should not be ungrateful. But I say that it is *NOT* nitpicking, and it *DOES* matter, and we *DID NOT* have a hit. If that makes me an ingrate, so be it. Something to tell your grandchildren? Pur-lease! In any case, I didn't write the song; *Deeply Dippy* was Right Said Fred's baby.

With the stars favourably aligned and with a little music in your soul you may write verses perhaps a dozen times in the course of your life – so the great blind Argentine once said. I have done stuff, good stuff it has been said, 12 albums in all, which is not a prodigious output, but it amounts to My Achievement. I have consoled myself that success is relative, but achievement is absolute. Commercially though, my songwriting and recording output has been *absolutely unsuccessful*. Have any other artists had so many comparable opportunities (records, publishing, TV, radio, good press and reviews, festivals and tours) and stuck around for as long as I have, who can show so woeful a return? Come on! Show them to me now. Bring the poor devils before me.

No, I do not think so. When it comes to being the British music industry's sub-cult status commercial disaster area unsurpassed, I have come to claim my prize.

This is not a tale of woe. Somebody has to be where I am, and my purpose here is to find out why it turned out to be me. I am most definitely not complaining. I am, indeed, A-OK. This is not the story of my life. My life has not been bad, but to recount it all would be ghastly. During the first Covid lockdown I wrote a diary for a few months. Somebody had suggested this was a good idea; it was not. The daily writing of it was torturous, and the reading of it later on was so great a chore I could only endure a few entries. How I wish I had spent all that diary writing time clearing out the loft and the little front bedroom.

What you have here is only that which is germane to my subject, and that subject is failure, *my* failure. Failure, after all is said and done, is not a tragedy, it is an everyday thing and the way of the world. It is, in other words, a comedy.

The D'Arcy Drive Sound

I WAS A Beatles baby, born in 1961, the fortunate son of loving parents, Dennis and Christina, a white-collar working dad and a stay-at-home mum. Our family doctor was a pipe-smoking Scot with an enthusiasm for delivering babies. Mum was happy to oblige him; my sister and I were born at home under the watch of Dr Thompson and the local midwife. I arrived first, blessed with bright ginger-red hair, and Alyson came two years later, blessed without it. Home was a three-bedroom terraced house in Kenton, Harrow, Middlesex, about 10 miles north of Trafalgar Square. Dad had bought it in 1959 from his best man, Alan Smith. Alan, Val and their young family were moving on to bigger and better things, but we never did. As I write it is still the family home.

I liked to watch television and listen to music. The first pop songs I remember singing along with were *She Loves You* and *I Want To Hold Your Hand,* which are nice songs for a little kid, when you think about it. At that early age I understood that drums are the most important instruments of all, so my first favourite group was the Dave Clark Five, whose drums were the loudest and the proudest.

In the 60s and 70s nearly every big singing star had their own show on TV: Cliff, Engelbert, Tom Jones, Cilla, Lulu, Roger Whittaker, even Scott Walker. You would watch them all unless there was something good on the other side; in those days there were only three TV channels, and our rented 405-line box only picked up two of them.

With my sister and our friend Julia, we formed our first pop group, Lulu's Children. We couldn't play anything and we didn't know any songs to sing, but our fantasy mum had her own television show, and in our game we would act out how she adoringly introduced us, how we received the studio audience's rapt attention with endearing giggles and smiles, and how we left the stage in humble triumph to rousing applause and a few cheers. Our performance in between consisted only of us bobbing about a bit and mouthing the words of imaginary songs into invisible microphones.

It wasn't long before we three were given our chance in a real show, albeit not the kind that we had fantasised about. Our parents did amateur operatics, and we appeared as 'the children' in *Gipsy Love*, a production by the Hendon Catholic Operatic Society (Amateur) that was performed for four nights running at the Hampstead Garden Suburb Institute in April, 1970.

Our part was to rush on stage excitedly and cry, "*Antonio's coming! Antonio's coming!*"

To which the leading man (Paddy Molloy) responded, arching his black-lined eyebrows in astonishment, "*What! With a lady?*"

And we gushed, in practised unison, "*No! All by himself!*"

In addition to reciting our lines we sang in the chorus, along with everyone else in the society that did not have a substantial speaking part. Chorus choreography was always quite uncomplicated: we all stood still in an arc behind the leading actors and sang up to the climax of each song, at which point we would collectively reach out our arms to the audience, before raising them above our heads at the end of the number, to demonstrate its conclusion.

I remember the smell and the feel of the greasepaint, if not the roar of the crowd. It really was greasepaint in those days; that old fashioned 'pancake' make-up required more grease to remove it, and Mum wasn't thorough about making sure I finished the job. I went to school the next day with some still on my face and neck, and the teasing I got from my classmates was probably my first experience of suffering for my art.

Operatics continued, on and off, through my childhood. I did not care for the music, because it was music for grown-ups, not the pop music I liked, but I went along nevertheless. In later years, on Thursday rehearsal nights, if I wasn't needed after the nine o'clock tea break, I would go out to the car and listen to Nicky Horne's nightly rock show, *Your Mother Wouldn't Like It*, on Capital Radio. Of all the productions we did, I quite liked *Oklahoma*. I remember Mum turning our house into a mini-costume factory, with hastily-made gingham shirts and dresses and other farmer and cowboy clobber strewn about, making the place even more untidy than it usually was. Obviously I owe my later country music inclinations to this influence.

Over the years I have become better disposed to musicals and opera than I was then, though I am picky about what I like. People often dismiss musical theatre because it is not realistic; nobody ever bursts into song at any available opportunity, they complain. As far as I am concerned, this is not a valid criticism of musicals, it is a criticism of real life. If people do not sing when they are reading the news, locking prisoners up, or performing surgery, then real life is so much the worse for it.

"Sing nicely or not at all" was a favourite saying of my mother's, and whenever I hear anything sung by Tom Waits I am reminded of it. We now make a great thing about taste, as if the having of it is somehow a measure of our merit. I remember it being said of a particular record company A&R guy we knew in the 90s that he had "such great *taste*". The thing is, people like my parents and their parents before them didn't much go in for taste. Anything appearing in sheet music, sung mellifluously and in tune and containing no profanities, was probably alright by them.

Grandad Joe, my mother's talented father, was known to be a fine singer (as was she). Despite being deafened by his injuries serving in the First World War, Joe Allen still entertained local audiences in song at concerts around Edgware and north west London, usually accompanied by Gladys (our nan) on piano. A boiler engineer by trade (he had been a corporal in the Royal Engineers) Joe was familiar to my sister and me mainly from a photograph that tends to take pride of place among the other family pictures. An explosion at work in 1959 had done for our grandad what the Germans had failed to do. Wanting to know more about him, I asked Mum to remember a song he liked to sing, and, after a moment's thought, she said *"Trees". Trees* was a very popular song in its time (I think it cropped up in a *Dad's Army* episode once) but it has to be said, *Trees* is an absolute stinker. Check out the version by Mario Lanza, or any other. Whatever dubious merit the original poem may have had is sapped by a ponderous tune.

> *"I think that I will never see,*
> *a poem lovely as a tree"*

I am sure Grandad Joe sang some very beautiful songs in his day, but I suspect he found joy in the indifferent stuff as he did in the good. Taste is a bourgeois construct which has gradually filtered down from the higher classes to the lower ones until nearly everyone is now afflicted with it. Taste gets us picking and choosing and discriminating and wanting new things. We might have been happier if we had remained innocent of the whole business.

*

My first brush with real fame came with being a choirboy. Originally drawing from a few schools in the London boroughs of Harrow and Brent, by 1972 the Pueri Cantores was made up only of boys from St Gregory's High School, the Catholic comprehensive where I had just started. A local priest, Father D, worked there as a music teacher, and he ran the choir.

Girls (according to Father D) had "tinny voices" and were not admitted. We boys enjoyed the male privilege of singing in the choir, but bribery also played a part in persuading us into those red cassocks with big white crosses around the necks. As well as being generous with school house points, Father D had his own choir house point system, which won you prizes (plastic footballs, toys, comics and whatever else) as rewards for attending practices during lunch hours and after school, and for distinguishing yourself by singing beautifully. His favourite choristers would also be taken out for treats. Though I was not one of the most favoured, I remember myself and some other boys tucking into enormous knickerbocker glories in a Golders Green ice cream parlour, all generously provided by our dog-collared guardian.

Then there were the foreign concert trips. In the first year a visit of several days to Austria was organised. I was not to go, I can't remember why, but I remember hearing the stern talk Father D gave before the lucky ones departed, warning them about the dangers of drinking (this was to boys of 11-13 years old). On a previous trip to Rome, one of his drunken choirboys had been taken to hospital to have his stomach pumped. There were no such mishaps this time, but my pals Sean Regan and Charles O'Malley came back with large tales of drinking sessions in the hotel bars and restaurants. I had missed out.

We sang masses and concerts and oratorios such as Handel's *Messiah* and Stainer's *Crucifixion*, which I particularly enjoyed. Then came our big break; we were invited to appear on the *Stars On Sunday* Christmas show on ITV. On a weekend in December, 1972, a coach-full of choirboys was taken up from north-west London to the Yorkshire TV studios in Leeds to record the show.

After being cleaned up, made up and be-cassocked, we were led into the giant TV studio and stood on a terrace all along one side. In the middle of the floor were three grand pianos that belonged to the well-known three grand piano act that was going to perform and accompany all the singers. This was impressive, but then, to my great excitement, the show's two star singing acts, the Beverley Sisters and Anita Harris, came in and stood over to our left. They were all smiles and celebrity loveliness, especially Anita, who looked directly up at us, waved exuberantly and gave me (I am *sure* of it) a conspiratorial wink.

On the other side of the pianos was Jess Yates, the show's host, who sat at his organ in his sacred-looking enclave in front of a stained glass panel. The Yorkshireman (father of doomed pop celeb

Paula Yates) was a well-known TV personality and producer, one of the big figures of popular TV entertainment. On *Stars On Sunday* he affected a simpering, grandfatherly persona which was presumed to appeal especially to the very young and to the very old. In his holy corner he would play his organ, introduce the acts, and read out requests for songs and hymns sent in by children and their older relatives and friends from all over the country (but especially from Yorkshire).

With everyone assembled, Jess stood up and issued a few warm words of welcome, thanking us all for being on his special Christmas show. But when he tried to settle down at his place to begin, something was not quite right, and after some moments of uneasy quiet, interspersed with a couple of bangs and then a louder crash, Jess exclaimed, "Somebody's kicked me microphone... and it's BOOGERED!"

At this we choirboys were shepherded out of the studio before any further references to sodomy could be made by our pious host.

Once reassembled, we sang a Christmas carol, and at the end we sang the choruses to the popular drinking song *Little Brown Jug* with the stars singing the verses, the three pianos thumping away, and Jess on the organ. Then it was back to London to wait for the broadcast, due the following weekend.

On that Sunday before Christmas, as the much-anticipated early evening programme approached, my family gathered excitedly round our black and white television set, with the pink fairy on the top of our white artificial Christmas tree also looking on. There was some nervousness about whether we were going to get a clear view of me. "Where's Alan?" they asked when the choir came on. "Where's Alan? Ooh! There he is. THERE!"

I was on the television.

Unfortunately I did not make it into the movies, as a few lucky choristers did. *Stardust,* released in 1974 and starring singer David Essex, had funeral scenes shot at a church in Northolt which featured half a dozen of us. I was disappointed not to be one of them, but was still interested to hear all about it afterwards from Anthony Curran and John Burke. David Essex was a really good bloke, they said, but Adam Faith was a grumpy bastard who shouted and swore at them for sitting on the bonnet of his Roller.

When the film came out we all went to see it, despite the AA certificate to keep us under-14s out. The story of the rise and downfall of rock star anti-hero Jim MacLaine made a great impression on me.

*

One thing that may have held me back in the course of my life is an over-developed moral sense. I don't think I flatter myself by saying that – it is just the way I am, and I have sometimes wished I had more of the devil in me, and have been envious of those who are bolder and braver. Also, in the end, I have succumbed to most of the sins and temptations that my conscience has at various times agonised over and warned me against, so it is so much the worse for me.

At home my religious upbringing was unconventional, neither strict nor doctrinaire. Being from a 'mixed marriage' (Mum baptised a Roman Catholic, Dad not) the authorities had initially kept me out of the 'better' Catholic school my parents wanted me to go to, but for some reason relented when I reached junior school age at seven. I was ill-prepared for what awaited me at St Bernadette's Primary. Mum had rarely if ever taken us to church and I didn't know the Hail Mary, the Our Father, or what a rosary was. Added to that, my first day at the new school arrived before my uniform had been acquired. Not wanting me to look untidy, Mum sent me in wearing my old Glebe School tie. Under the pained gaze of Jesus on the cross some classmates turned on me and called me cross-eyed and a "Glebe-ite". Until then life had been untroubled and taken on trust: I believed in Father Christmas, clowns were funny, and I knew nothing of sexual intercourse. The beginning of my fall from happy innocent to disillusioned malcontent I trace precisely to that moment.

My new school awakened me to the reality of hierarchy. Kids here almost never interacted with children in other classes, and among the 20 boys in my class of 40 (there were two in each year) status was largely decided according to athleticism; how fast you could run. The playtime chasing game of Crocodile immediately revealed to all that running was not my strength, and so I was always one of the first to be caught, and among the last to be picked for any team. At the end of my first year, my participation in the summer sports day fun was short-lived; I came last in my sack race, last in the egg and spoon, last in a sprint, and that was my lot. I was out, my lowly ranking confirmed.

It felt a little harsh, but I did not dignify my lack of sporting talent by not caring, as other children not good at games sensibly did. I cared considerably, and liked sports of all kinds: football, cricket, athletics, Wimbledon fortnight, the Olympic Games... With the exception of Eddie Waring's dreary rugby league broadcast every Saturday on *Grandstand,* I watched everything going on the telly, and knew all the stars on *A Question Of Sport.*

Football was my favourite. Lots of boys at school supported Leeds United, who back then were the dominant English club. It took me a few seasons to decide who I would support, but eventually I stuck with Chelsea after following them to their FA Cup Final replay victory in 1970 (over Leeds, of course). I had longed to play the game for real, and at St Bernadette's I had my opportunity. Out on the full-size pitch where we played in the park next to the school, I knew enough about tactics not to join the snake-like procession of boys who chased the ball wherever it went. Cannily I stood out on the left wing, just onside by the half-way line, waiting for the ball to come my way. It was a long wait, but when my chances finally came I fluffed them so woefully that my team-mates learned not to trouble me further. And so I stood there, in my red jersey, dubbined boots and unmuddied white shorts, week after week, watching the game go by, like an unmoved man on my Waddingtons Table Soccer game. If only a teacher, or someone, had shouted at me to stop day-dreaming and get stuck in, I am sure I should have done so, but they never did, and so I never did.

Before reaching secondary school age, I was observing with mounting disapproval that the stricter Roman Catholic upbringing of my peers had no noticeably improving effect upon them. I resolved to do better, to observe the sacraments *and* be good, though with no encouragement to keep to it coming from either of my parents, the former resolve (going to church each Sunday and regular confessions) did not last long.

Mum was a Catholic because her family had converted when her father got a job in a convent school; her commitment to Catholicism was not fervent. Dad was a Protestant, and also a white collar trade unionist with an atheistic streak; "I'm a heretic", he would sometimes say. His family had been in the Salvation Army. His father, a door-to-door insurance man, played tenor horn in the Chalk Farm Army Band, but his highly-strung mum grew weary of Salvationism and Ted and Elsie Tyler had gone over to the Methodists for a quieter life. Though Dad had wanted me to go to a Catholic school, he still nursed some of the English anti-Catholic sentiment that was common then and all but forgotten now. I remember he once ripped down a "This Is Holy Week" poster Mum had uncharacteristically put in the front window. Perhaps this mixture of weak Catholicism and Protestant nonconformism (if that is a correct way to describe it) did something to prompt and then confuse my overactive moral compass.

My quest for values found an unlikely outlet in pop music. I wasn't content to listen to what was in the charts and just enjoy it (though I did, a lot). I started to take music *seriously*, and wanted to make *good* choices. In the early to mid 70s there was still only

BBC Radio 1 playing pop music, and this was very singles chart-based, which was great, of course; it was the golden era of British pop, but I wanted more. I sometimes listened to Alan Freeman's Saturday afternoon rock show, and there was also John Peel's show, but that was late at night and too esoteric, even for adventurous me. Independent commercial radio (in London, Capital Radio) still hadn't come along. In theory there were Radio Luxembourg and Caroline, but the reception in Kenton was too poor to listen to either.

If you didn't have an older brother or sister or know other kids who had records, your opportunities to listen to them were not great. The newly-opened Harrow record library was mainly classical, with a smattering of jazz and folk (I managed to borrow *John Wesley Harding* by Bob Dylan, a Ralph McTell album, and Miles Davis's *Bitches Brew*). Not being a particularly sociable or popular kid, 'inclined to solitude' you might say, with no wide circle of family or friends, and little money for records, I took to reading about what I couldn't get to hear.

One treasury of information was the *NME Book Of Rock,* a single, fat paperback volume that I bought from Woolworth's in 1975. It was an A-Z encyclopaedia of all the main known groups and artists (pop, rock, blues, soul, country and a few jazzers), with a chronological list of albums at the end of each entry and numerous photographs in the middle. I referred to it constantly and soaked all the information up like a sponge.

I was also reading music magazines. I spent some holiday money on a copy of *Music Scene* and remember reading in it that David Bowie was a fan of Lou Reed and Iggy Pop. I had not heard of either before, but I marvelled at their strange names and cut out their pictures for my scrapbook. I was sure that they were amazing, even without hearing them, and I was right, of course.

But not always. My early trust in the wisdom of rock scribes induced some pretentiousness and wrong turns. I began to incline towards 'rock' and 'progressive' and eschew 'commercial pop'. I wrote "YES", "LED ZEP" and "GENESIS" in bubble letters on my school exercise books, copying a few older boys who did the same, who may even have properly heard these mysterious doyens of the 'underground'. I had barely listened to any of it. Fortunately, something much better was around the corner that would steer me off the progressive path before I had gone a long distance down it.

*

The time came to learn to play guitar. I answered an advert in the music shop window in Edgware, placed by a local lass who was still at school, and who taught folk and classical. Annoyingly, Mum decided she wanted to learn too, and as she was paying, we both went along with our newly-bought £15 classical guitars and squeezed into Ruth Lever's sweet-smelling boudoir.

Happily, Mum's learning did not progress beyond her second lesson. She refused to trim her fingernails short enough to navigate the fretboard, so I was left alone with Ruth to learn the chords of *Feelin' Groovy*. Ruth was only a couple of years older than me, but was bossy enough to make her a plausible teacher, and keep me very much at arm's length. She had a white stereo record player with a smoky Perspex lid – the kind that I wanted, not having a record player of my own. All her records were leant up next to it, with Dory Previn's *Mythical Kings And Iguanas* placed prominently at the front of them. I wondered what it was like, and whether I'd like it. When I got home my *NME Book Of Rock* told me it was "naked sensitivity laced with traces of wry humour".

Ruth had more records than I. I had *Don't Shoot Me I'm Only The Piano Player* (Elton John), *Miles Of Aisles* (Joni Mitchell), *Dark Side Of The Moon* (Pink Floyd), *No Reason To Cry* (Eric Clapton), *Birth Of A Success* (a cheap Jimi Hendrix on Music For Pleasure records) and a Duke Ellington album I got from Woolies for 50p, which I still listen to. I also had some cassettes that I could listen to in my room: *Goodbye Yellow Brick Road* (Elton John), *461 Ocean Boulevard* (Eric Clapton) and *Trilogy* by Emerson, Lake & Palmer, who my dad called Emerson, Lake & Crumpet, as a joke. I liked Elton John best of all. This was because, obviously, he was good, but also because he was from Pinner, near where I lived, and I liked the idea that someone who lived near where I lived could be a star.

*

In 1976 my musical judgement confronted its most radical test. For a brief few weeks I took an ethical stand against punk rock, agreeing with Radio 1 DJ Johnny Walker that it was "musical rubbish" and a disgrace. But I soon found myself stealing guilty listens to the fast and frantic rock noise of The Damned's *New Rose* and the Sex Pistols' *Anarchy In The UK* whenever they came on the radio or TV. It was irresistible, and I soon succumbed to the vitality and excitement of punk. I was all in.

Since the beginning of 1976 I had been buying *Sounds*, the weekly music paper, and I was now tracking every new band and every new record that came out. At first I trusted the sensible opinions of journalists like Barbara Charone and Phil Sutcliffe, but before the year was out I was picking out pieces and reviews by the more active champions of the new wave: Jane Suck, Giovanni Dadomo, Jonh Ingham and Sandy Robertson. Dadomo went over the top and gave *The Modern Lovers* a 10 stars out of five album review. His word was good enough for me; I went to Virgin in Marble Arch that weekend, forked out for the "*Home of the Hits*" original on import, and it changed my life.

Loads of records were changing my life; everything was changing. A new edition of my beloved *NME Book Of Rock* was now nigh on impossible. It had been updated in 1976 with just a few amendments, adding the albums and the handful of acts (like Deaf School and Racing Cars) that had come out the year before. But by

1977 the number of new bands that had appeared was incredible, and would require a whole new book, if such a book could be written quickly enough, because bands were springing up every week. The *Book Of Rock* was obsolete, and most of the old bands in it suddenly seemed passé.

Or at least, so it seemed for me. It all made little impression on the kids at school, who carried on wearing flares and listening to the same old stuff, going to discos as if nothing else was happening. But I was completely carried away, and had my own money from Saturday and holiday jobs to buy records and save up for an electric guitar. During 'free periods' I would walk out of school and take the long number 52 bus ride from Kingsbury to Rough Trade Records near Portobello Road, which became the centre of my universe. And I was going to gigs: small venues like the Marquee in Soho and the Nashville Rooms in West Kensington didn't seem to care if you were underage, and I went to see so many bands at these places, and at sometimes bigger ones like the Hammersmith Odeon, the Lyceum and the Electric Ballroom.

Nearly always I went alone, because nobody at school seemed interested. The exception was my bespectacled schoolmate Colin McKane, who ventured out with me a few times, and then, when he left school, I met Bowie-loving Gail Sherwood from the year below me, and we swapped a few records and went to see Iggy Pop at the Lyceum one Sunday night with a few others from the lower sixth. Other than that, I was on my own, and I demonstrated my differentness by pulling my school tie into a tight knot (a la Tom Robinson), rather than having it fat like everyone else, and by wearing a moth-eaten jumper with a big hole in it.

Bands I went to see in the next couple of years, often on multiple occasions, included Alternative TV, The Fall, The Mekons, The Radio Stars, The Human League, DAF, The Slits, Cabaret Voltaire, Crass, Gang of Four, The Scars, The Monochrome Set, The Raincoats, Felt, Stiff Little Fingers, Spizz Oil, Throbbing Gristle,

Buzzcocks, Pigbag, Subway Sect, The Blue Orchids, The Barracudas, The Pop Group, A Certain Ratio, Scritti Politti, The Birthday Party, The Rezillos and The Revillos. Of the American bands I liked, apart from Iggy, I got to see The Cramps (who did a tour with The Fall), Pere Ubu, Nico and Jonathan Richman & The Modern Lovers at the Hammersmith Odeon both times they came over to play there.

Punk brought its own set of ethical and political prerogatives, which I was bound to consider with greater earnestness than most, and this put me against a few of the groups. Joe Strummer's elevated class background was perhaps a lame reason for not liking The Clash, but it sufficed for me. The band were also guilty of signing to CBS, a major record label, which was a no-no for all the truly hardcore punk ethicists. Of these, Crass were in the vanguard; these Epping Forest commune dwellers were uncompromisingly indie, anti-corporate and anti-profit, but I could take them no more seriously than The Clash. *Do They Owe Us A Living?,* their great anarchist anthem to entitlement, had an unintended comic effect on me that always brought a wry smirk to my face (as it does still). I found myself in neither the Crass nor the Clash camp when it came to signing to majors, but I certainly thought being on Small Wonder or Rough Trade was more noble than compromising with EMI or Warners.

It was so much bullshit. Experience was to show me that small labels were less bound by the rule-book and were at least as capable of sharp practice and ripping off musicians as the big boys. Rough Trade's deal with The Smiths, which gave Morrissey and Johnny Marr bigger slices of the pie than bandmates Mike Joyce and Andy Rourke, was a shocking case in point. What made it all the worse was that Rough Trade boasted of being a collective where workers were all paid the same wage. The part played by Morrissey and Marr in the deal has sometimes been criticised, but the hypocrisy of the label goes ignored. The reason: people in the music business avoid speaking of such things, because to criticise the business practices of others would only invite scrutiny of your own, and where is the profit in that? In the music business, everyone likes to stay sweet with everybody else (or, at least, to keep up that appearance). Nobody wants to upset the honey pot – even those who have been badly stung know to stay close, in the hope that the sweet stuff will come their way another day.

I resisted Joy Division, suspicious of their dalliance with Nazi-era imagery. I also thought they were too obvious, a distillation of so much else that was going on at that time; now I think that's what made them good. One band would toy with existential angst (The Cure), another with The Gothic (Bauhaus) and others with modernism (any number of electronic bands), but Joy Division fused these elements and nailed them into an obsessive unity. I have always been inclined to 'do something different', but it is good to go with the mood of the epoch, if you do it single-mindedly and with full commitment, as they did.

From the earliest I was always very in favour of girl groups, and female participation in general. Women should be more included, I thought, and musicians like Tina Weymouth in Talking Heads and Mo Tucker in the Velvets seemed to bring something distinct and special to their bands. I adored the oblique, punky inventions of The Slits, The Raincoats, and Kleenex. Not all the girl bands were good, of course; I didn't like them all. One of them I blame for permanent damage to my left eardrum when I stood too close to the PA speaker while they shrieked a Janis Joplin song for an encore. I won't say who they were.

I later revised my opinion, taking the reluctance of girls to be in bands with us boys as a sign of their good sense. It is irrelevant now, of course. With the old up-escalator for new bands now broken down, the mainly male efforts to climb it that I'll describe in my story belong to a bygone era.

*

Nobody in my family had ever been to university. One night my parents came back excitedly from the school open evening to tell me that Miss Binks, my science teacher, had said I was an excellent student, and I should think about doing A-levels and going on to do a degree. This was pleasing but unexpected news. I was surprised, because Miss Binks never paid any particular attention to me in class. I quietly wondered whether she had muddled me up with someone else.

Over time though, I did OK at school, and I went on to pass all my exams quite well, winning the right to a place at university. My teachers didn't think much of me in class, for the most part, but I had a knack of doing better in exams than they expected, while their classroom favourites often came up short. Good for me, you may say. Yes, it was – but since then experience has taught me that it is usually a greater advantage in life to be dim-witted but considered bright, than it is to be... well, whatever I'm like.

When the time came, I decided that I wasn't quite ready to go to university, and I would "take a year out". This would have dismayed my parents had I not already disappointed them with my decision to study Performing Arts at Ilkley College, an eccentric choice of school and subject. They were probably right in thinking my prospects of finding gainful employment after going there were as bleak as the moor on which it stood. Part of Ilkley's attraction for me was its fully-equipped recording studio, which was a rare thing in a seat of learning back then. But anyway, university didn't happen. I had things I wanted to do where I was.

My first move was to write a fanzine. I called it *Cool*. The title was an exercise in intentional contrariness. I knew I wasn't cool, but I wanted to achieve a certain coolness, by not trying to be cool, by not doing the cool thing.

In part I took as my exemplar and inspiration Jonathan Richman, who was already challenging his 'prince of punk' legacy with Blakean songs about angels and dinosaurs played at low volumes on acoustic instruments. In the UK we had the emerging Swell Maps, who combined overdriven riffing and DIY home recording with poetic, Bolanesque lyrics and an iconography plundering children's TV and literature. The inventively-named members of the group were Nikki Mattress (soon to be Nikki Sudden), Epic Soundtracks, Jowe Head, Phones B Sportsman, Golden Cockrill, and Biggles Books.

Swell Maps invited correspondence by putting their home address in Solihull on the picture sleeve of their first single, *Read About Seymour*. Under my own, newly-invented *nom de guerre*,

Alan T Wireless, I sent them questionnaires (what's your favourite record, TV programme, etc) which they soon returned to me, to my great delight, in a package bejewelled with coloured stars and glitter and bursting with little toys and cuttings, along with additional replies from Mayo Thompson of the Red Crayola (their producer) and Sue Mailorder, who worked at Rough Trade.

Cool (20p) came out in September 1979. My master copy, part-typed and part hand-rendered, I had taken to Joly, a beneficent hippy who ran Better Badges from his printing shop at the top of Portobello Road. Flicking through the final product that he'd faithfully printed for me, Joly gave his assessment, page by page: the Swell Maps questionnaires ("good"), a story about President Carter's boat being attacked by rabbits ("quite funny"), an article about living in Harrow ("a bit harrowing")…

I didn't have to pay him anything; his only stipulation was the two-page Better Badges ad (listing badges, T-shirts, other fanzines and a few bootleg tapes he sold by mail order) was inserted. I was happy. I got most of the 500 printed copies to sell myself, and he put the others in a few shops.

I shifted quite a few to people in queues at gigs before getting lazy about it. A younger lad who lived next door to me, Sunil, got wind of my creation, and offered to sell them at his school. I was sceptical, but I gave him a pile, and in a single day he had sold them all. Impressed at my enterprise, his dad, Mr Mistri, invited me into their house to congratulate me. I agreed to give Sunil some more to sell, but this time I handed over copies that didn't have the Better Badges ad. He came back from school the next day, having sold precisely none. It was badges that the kids at his school were hungry for, not my writerly wit.

Other people did read it, though, and some of them wrote to me, from all over. One of them, significantly, lived in Kenton, not far from me. Paul Platypus (née Rosen) was a diminutive sixth-form schoolboy with considerably greater beard growth than I, who still wore the clothes his mum bought for him. He too had been writing to the Swell Maps and was already in a band called Exhibit A that he had formed with some chums at their private school in leafy Highgate. Paul was the one-year-younger brother of Jeremy, who had been in my class at Glebe School infants. Paul and Jeremy had a little sister, a pretty, good natured mum (called Wendy, who I was a little sweet on) and a dad who did a lot of complaining, "Pau-aul, for the last time, will you turn that music down PLEEEEASE?"

Paul invited me round to their house at 7 D'Arcy Drive to record some "silly songs". Being, as I have mentioned, serious about music, I baulked at the "silly". I liked all the mad Swell Mappian kids' TV references and esoteric naming, but the Exhibit A efforts were rather less exotic and, I thought, more just plain schoolboy silliness (Irrelevant Wombat Records, Andrew Lunchbox – hmmmm). But I kept schtum about my misgiving, and went along. It was a minor quibble; Platypus was the only person I knew who liked music I liked, wanted to make some himself, and lived just down the road.

So we settled down in his bedroom. Platypus plugged his guitar into his amp, and I sat with one of those tambourines with a drum skin on, holding two drumsticks, ready to beat time and sing. A portable cassette recorder was on the floor between us, the condenser mic primed and ready to go.

"What shall we call this one?" I asked.

"You are a fish," said Platypus.

At this, Paul hit the record button and began strumming. I picked up the tempo on the tambourine, and launched into the unknown.

> *"You are a fish....*
> *....slimy and cold,*
> *A fish you are...,*
> *...you are a fish.*

> *Well I don't like you...*
> *...'cos you are a fish,*
> *A fish you are...*
> *....you are a fish.*
> *There's something fishy going on,*
> *And I've decided it must be* YOU*!"*

After the concluding *j'accuse* of this singular verse, we progressed with much drum bashing and guitar thrashing. I added a few more made-up rhymes, and then we fashioned an ending to our song, by stopping. Feeling my powers of spontaneous lyric composition were now exhausted, I picked up my guitar, and we contrived four meandering instrumentals before ending our recording session.

Greatly satisfied, we took considerable delight in what we had created. I had a copy that I listened to at home, over and over. Our recording process was repeated a couple more times, until we had enough for Paul to compile an album, which we called *The Demonstrable Index Of Kalsity* under the name of The Amsterdam 5. This we 'released' on cassette with double-sided A4 photocopied artwork with copious sleeve notes that we folded over and squeezed into the case with the cassette.

Aversion to silliness means I will not bore you with exhaustive details of the strange names we invented for our fictitious Amsterdam 5, nor the elaborate backstory we made up about the album's surreptitious recording conducted by disgruntled Dutch record execs who sought recompense for large advances squandered by the elusive and now comatose musicians kept alive on expensive life support machines. I will only add that the title of the album is a misread quote of one of the answers Mayo Thompson had scrawled on his *Cool* fanzine questionnaire. It was "demonstrable index of falsity", not kalsity.

My world expanded with other fanzine writers and DIY music makers who wrote to me and shared their stuff. Beaver the

Postman (Paul Beveridge) from Rainham in Essex did *Crash Smash Crack Ring* fanzine and already had a considerable DIY tape output, *Posing At The Scala Vol. 3* being his latest. Beaver was the son of Johnny Bev from Joe Brown and the Bruvvers, and Cliff Richard had been his childhood family friend; Beaver had some old home movies to prove it. Bill Popstar from Portsmouth did a fanzine – I'm damned if I can remember what it was called now; I lost most of my old fanzines and letters in a house move years later. Rob Callous was in a Crass-like punk band called Six Minute War who had put out two EPs ("PAY ONLY 50p FOR THIS RECORD") but he was also game for the experimental DIY stuff. Ant Insect (Tony Davis) was from Pinner and had drawn and forwarded me some cartoon strips to go into my next fanzine. He also played drums, owned the Mustang bass that we used to tune up to, and had a car. Together we would gather on Saturday mornings at Alleyway rehearsal studio in Fulham Broadway, plug in to the house amps and make an electrified racket, recording everything and listening to it avidly on the way home to pick out "good bits".

Of course, we were not very good. But not being very good, so we thought (or at least, so *I* thought) made us good; we were not hindered or inhibited by the expertise that afflicted "proper musicians". We were free and authentic.

The "anyone can do it" DIY/punk ethos of the late 70s gave me the temerity to thrust myself forward into pop, but my zealous over-adherence to it, then and in later years, has also held me back. *Sideburns* fanzine drew the chord window boxes of A, E, and G and said "This is a chord... this is another... this is a third... now join a band". I took this as my article of faith, and never fully shook off that unhelpful attitude. People like Mark Perry of *Sniffin' Glue* and Alternative TV fame hadn't told me to play scales, practice hard, and learn tonal intervals to improve my ability to play by ear, so I didn't move on to assemble the basic skills that would have made me a more rounded and competent musician.

The reality was, most of the great people who started off inept, like Jonathan Richman, got better, a lot better, and this was something I wasn't caring to acknowledge. Sure, the primal three-chord "peaking on the meter" thrash of The Mekons' single *Where Were You* is still hard to beat, but most of the innovative bands I loved around that time could really play and were always advancing. But I clung to my untutored primitivism, as exemplified by the Maps, ATV, Throbbing Gristle and, to an extent, The Fall. Learning and improving I thought petit bourgeois and unimaginative. I was wedded to the Cult Of The Can't, whilst marvelling at those who could, not knowing quite how they did it.

I was bloody daft.

Or perhaps not completely daft. Perhaps my can't-do attitude was a fig leaf for a genuine innate ineptitude. Left-handed and decidedly cack-handed, I was not as hopeless as some, but still... I was passable at singing, but have never been clever with my hands. I could master the early basics of guitar with little trouble, but more advanced skills seemed as far out of my power as leaping 12 feet up into the air. No amount of practice and application would coordinate my brain and the fingers of both hands to produce a guitar solo, and consequently I have never played one. I can strum acoustic guitar competently and in time, and fingerpick a little, but that, I am afraid, is your lot. Though not a "non-musician" as Brian Eno has claimed to be, I am at best a partial one. No-one would have me in their band... no-one sensible, anyway.

The downside of my aversion to technique was amply illustrated by my first experience in a recording studio. I had decided to gather my fanzine friends together to record some of my embryonic songs that we had captured on cassette. Street Level Studios was the HQ of Fuck Off Records, a DIY/punky/hippy label associated with some not terribly well-known groups (now or then), Danny & The Dressmakers, The Instant Automatons, and the 012s. But the house engineer was Grant Showbiz, who did have musical credibility; we had seen him doing the sound at Fall gigs, and he had produced the great band's latest record, *Dragnet*. He, and cheapness, were the great attractions of Street Level.

Platypus and I took a trip on the tube to have a look. One stop from the familiar, fashionable and relatively safe Ladbroke Grove, Latimer Road felt desolate and post-apocalyptic. We turned out of the station and there was hardly any traffic. Travellers' caravans were parked on some waste land, probably an old bomb site. A bony stray dog went by. On the other side of the road decrepit old men stood outside a huge, stark, uninviting old pub. On our side, boarded-up shop fronts outnumbered the open establishments. One of these was our destination.

> Record your independent single/
> album/cassette
> at
> **STREET LEVEL**
> ★ DISGUSTING TOILET!
> ★ HORRIBLE BACK YARD!
> ★ CRAZY ENGINEERS!
> ★ AIR-CONDITIONING!
> ★ 8 TRACK ONE INCH AMPEX!
> ★ FANTASTIC SOUND!
> "Simply the coolest
> Studio in town" (MARTIN ATOMS)
> special £6.50 p.hr. Readers
> Fanzine rate!
> ·7337 ★ 289·9699

We rang the bell, and after a while a sleepy-looking hippy woman came and let us in. We announced our business to her, and she disappeared into the back, leaving us in the shop area, which was full of car parts, old machinery and other junk. As we waited, there was a stirring from underneath a pile of debris in the corner, from which emerged Kif Kif Le Batteur, the drummer of Here & Now, who I recognised from the group photo on the back of the

Alternative TV/Here & Now live album *What You See... Is What You Are,* one of my favourite records at the time. Kif Kif must have been having a sleep.

Grant Showbiz came up and showed us the studio, and let me use their notoriously disgusting and ancient toilet, which had a bucket of water next to it for flushing. Grant was delightfully friendly and massively enthusiastic. He played us a recording he was mixing, *I'm Free* by The Petticoats, a version of the Who song, and we agreed that it was absolutely *GREAT*. A date for our recording was booked in.

The group that assembled for the session was, I think, me, Platypus, Beaver, and Ant on drums. Perhaps there was another playing bass, but more likely that was Beaver. The plan was to do my occult-inspired *Witches Song,* followed by a more free-form wig-out, *My Guitar Is Powered By Gas.*

As per our rehearsal recording (which I had been mightily satisfied with), *The Witches Song* began with a solo spoken word introduction. Self-conscious in the studio setting, I nervously began, trying to assume the required demonic tone:

"Urbain Grandier, you have been tried and found guilty of witchcraft by this jury, and I now pass sentence upon you..."

At which point Platypus came in with the song's Fall-like down and up guitar figure, and then I sang:

> *"There are witches in this town*
> *Some are white and some are brown"*

The guitar line was repeated, and then:

> *"There was a girl in love with me*
> *But she pissed off to Italy"*

Now, on our rehearsal tape, Platypus's guitar line came in once again, and that was followed by more emphatic riffing and the occasional vocal ad lib, much like our earlier Amsterdam 5 fish opus. But in the studio we were all too inhibited and unsure to carry even this through with any conviction, and the attempt fizzled out without having much fizz in the first place. Having failed to provide my musicians with a song that had a middle or an end, the take collapsed.

Vainly I looked to Grant for production guidance. I expect he smiled encouragingly and suggested we try it again, but my recollections have disappeared into the fog of disappointment that descended on me once my bubble of optimism had burst. It wasn't working, it wasn't going to work, and no, I did *not* want to have another go. Maybe we did try again, or we tried the other song; I can't remember. I just remember leaving in umbrage. I think Paul came away with a tape, Grant may have "mixed" something, but I was never going to listen to it.

I was surely not the first or the last to have toiled under a misconception, which is to imagine that recording studios make what you do sound wonderful. In fact, of course, despite the gadgets and trickery at your disposal, in essence a good studio makes you sound exactly like what you sound like, with great fidelity. It was all clear to me now, abundantly and horribly clear.

Obviously as well, the song, insofar as it qualified as a song at all, was cobblers.

I have so far neglected to tell you that the band name for this inauspicious debut recording was The Fire Engines. What's in a name? You may ask. Everything, I will always answer. We were always making up new band names. Every rehearsal begat a new one: Birdlife UK, The Sissy Spacek Band, The Candy Clark Band... The Fire Engines I thought such a tremendous name that I registered it at the Registry of Business Names, and kept the certificate in a drawer. My legal claim was worth next to nothing, I was soon to learn. In Edinburgh, Davy Henderson had a Fire Engines as well, presumably inspired, as I was, by an unreleased song by our New York heroes, Television.

Red, resounding, urgent, angular and art, the real Fire Engines were everything I wanted our band to be like. So much more skilled a guitarist than I, Henderson summoned the thunder and lightning that we had failed to conjure up in Street Level, despite my absurd occult incantation. I didn't really mind, I bloody loved The Fire Engines. At least I'd had the same idea... kind of.

Later I returned to Grant's studio to record with The Jelly Babies, Beaver's group. This went more successfully, because Beaver was more of a realist than I was. He finished writing his songs and had a flair for juicy chordplay on his recently-acquired Rickenbacker. A track from the resulting *De Nada EP,* called *Rollerskate,* got aired on The John Peel Show. More silly songs, though. It was time to put away these childish things.

Swing Gently

AFTER THE SWELL Maps shocked our world and split in 1980, Nikki Sudden did a solo single on Rough Trade, and our *Breach Of The Peace* fanzine-writing friend Robert Dellar offered him a gig at an all-dayer he was organising in a Watford youth club. Nikki honoured us by having us as his backing band. This was me, Platypus, and Andrew the drummer out of Exhibit A. Various Hertfordshire bands also played, including Sad Lovers & Giants, Soft Drinks, and Tracey Thorn's first group, Marine Girls.

But the gig with Nikki was a one-off that would go no further, a fact that was acknowledged without needing to be said. For one thing, we didn't look right. I had started to invest in my outfits, combining secondhand threads with purchases from Jack Geach, a Wealdstone tailor who had been kitting out the teddy boys and rockers in Harrow since the 50s. There I got a pair of pointy royal blue suede shoes with DM AirWair soles, dayglo pink socks, black pegs, and a couple of polka dot shirts, which I rounded off with an old paisley cravat that Dad never wore. With a leather car coat over the top, I was trying to be like the Flamin' Groovies looking dandy on the cover of *Jumpin' In The Night*. But whether my efforts were cutting it or not, Nikki's louche stylings were definitely never going to find their setting with sensibly-dressed Andrew Lunchbox and the anti-fashion Platypus, who still had gloves on elastic in the arms of his anorak.

Our cheap guitars were another fail. I had started with a reasonable Sakura Strat copy (as recommended in *Sounds*), but was now favouring a Westbury electric, a copy of I knew not what. Platypus still scratched at his weedy-sounding Argos catalogue electric. Nikki cut a dash with a new Gibson, the same kind that Johnny Thunders played. He had recently returned from hanging out with the legendary punk rock originator, on a quest to taste all the highs and lows that New York City had to offer.

I did two more fanzines. The centrepiece of *Cool #2* (February 1980) was an interview with The Fall. I had stood at the front at so many Fall gigs that I had assumed nodding terms with the band. Now I had a tape of me speaking to them, which I had written down for other people to read.

Dad worked for British Airways, and in those days BA staff could get flights for themselves and their families for next to nothing, so in April 1980 I booked a ticket to Newark, NJ and, following in Nikki Sudden's footsteps, took my blue suede shoes to New York City. Avoiding the punk rock establishments that Nikki would have frequented – Max's Kansas City and CBGB's – I headed instead for new funky club venues like Danceteria, The Ritz and The Mudd Club, where you could dance every night to records like *You're So Good* by ESG and *Shack Up* by A Certain Ratio. I saw gigs by Alan Vega, Hi Sheriffs Of Blue, The Wallets, Blurt, and James White (aka James Chance) who I was especially smitten with. I wrote about them all in *Cool #3*.

For a short time I was in a band in Grimsby called the Chain of Dots (COD – the acronym punned a little painfully on the prime catch of the port town's fishing industry). Their main man, Garry Baily, had got in touch after I had placed a classified ad in the *New Musical Express*. Placed under "musicians wanted", I composed it to read like a lonely heart:

> **"CONFUSED BOY** *guitarist seeks people for noises, dancing and romance. Please phone Alan 01-907-xxxx".*

Grimsby promised all the romance I wanted; I was attracted by the mystique of the north that bands like The Fall had cultivated, and was keen to venture up there and give the Chain of Dots a go.

The *Coronation Street*-style terraced house where Garry lived with his mum, dad and sister was even smaller than our one in Kenton, and had no garden to speak of. We shared interests in the electronic bands from Sheffield, the Manchester Factory bands, and Hackney art provocateurs Throbbing Gristle. Garry was going to get a synthesiser, but was agonising over which one. Moog synths were the best-known, Korgs were supposed to be good, and the new Wasp, with its non-moving keyboard, was the cheapest. "But are Wasps *really* any good?" we debated. I had no idea, never having laid hands on a synthesiser in my life.

Garry talked a good talk. There was a lot of talking before, during and after the rehearsal, but not much playing. Garry couldn't play anything.

I was the guitarist. The bass player of the Chain of Dots was Michael Clark (not the famous, dancing one, but similarly fair-haired and artistic-looking). We also had a singer, I can't remember her name at all, I only met her once. She lived on the other side of the Humber estuary, in Hull. She came over to Grimsby on the ferry (it was before the bridge was built), and we picked her up in Michael's car, on a Sunday morning, to take her to the rehearsal. She was quite a doll, with high heels, a pencil skirt, a bit of fur, make-up and a sexy northern accent. In the car, we talked about music. Our singer had been to see Generation X in the week. Those prancing punk pretenders were out of favour, as far as the boys in our band were concerned; too commercial.

"You don't like Gen X, do you?" Garry asked her, a little reproachfully.

"Nuurrrr..." said our singer, frowning a little as she corrected herself, before brightening again and announcing with unguarded relish: "...but I like Bully Idol!"

I caught Michael's eye in the rear-view mirror as we both glanced skywards.

I remember the first two lines (probably the only two lines) of the one song we tried, which Garry sought further input for development – he was also still at the 'starting songs but not finishing them' stage.

> *"I am like a catalyst in a jungle*
> *Waiting for the logical move..."*

The logical move was... nowt. The next time I went up, Michael, who I later learned was wavering in commitment, overslept. Arriving on a bleak and windy Sunday morning to find nobody there to meet her in Grimsby, our singer got straight back onto the ferry home to Hull.

*

A magnet for me in 1980 was the London Musicians Collective, which was in Gloucester Road, in the Primrose Hill part of Camden. The LMC brought together proper musicians, non-musicians, experimentalists and diverse musical boundary pushers; Steve Beresford and David Toop were leading lights. I went to several gigs there. At one, I saw Take It, a band I took a great shine to. Like the Raincoats they had a girl drummer (Else) with a unique, effervescent style. They were fronted by Igor (real name Steve

Wright), a tall, gangling chap in a green and yellow comedy check jacket who had some interesting lyrics. "This is a band I would love to be in," I declared.

Time passed, and I carried on going to all the gigs I could, with Platypus and Ant, mostly. Sometimes we hooked up with Ant's pal from Burnt Oak, Jim Reid. He was an entertaining companion who passionately desired to write for the *NME*, but ended up jobbing for *Record Mirror* and *Smash Hits* and was last heard of witnessing the KLF burning a million quid on the island of Jura. Ant would drive us all around in his Mini. It was not terribly wise; he liked a beer as much as Jim and I did, with Platypus the only sober one, sticking to his limit of just one "sweet cider".

I had a place waiting for me at Kent University to study Politics, starting in autumn 1980. In the meantime I got myself a job. It was easy then (in London, at least); numerous employment agencies advertised in the *Evening Standard*. You just had to ring one up, pop in their office and they'd send you to work somewhere. I settled for a time as a messenger for a firm of architects, delivering letters and drawings to building sites and offices around Central London. Each morning the head messenger gave his young runners cash to buy travel passes to get around. After a while, I had connected the proximity of the streets and squares of London in my mind, walked nearly everywhere, and was pocketing the fare money.

My London beat stretched from an office on Marylebone Road down to St Mary Axe, a City construction site on the edge of the East End. It was a distance of three miles or so, often much added to by my daily meanderings. Architects in Ferguson House, Portland Place and Great Portland Street produced drawings which I took to the dingy company print room in Cleveland Street. This was in the less salubrious environs of Fitzrovia, in a now demolished triangle of industrial units in between concrete council flats and the Post Office Tower. The drawings were transferred onto great sheets of tracing paper by a large machine in an enclosed atmosphere heavy with the reek of ammonia. The guys who worked there all day seemed cheerful enough, a bit wide-eyed perhaps, but I was always glad to get out of there into the fresher air to deliver my scrolls to contractors at prestige developments in Piccadilly and Petty France.

Outside, just around the corner, the Warren Street used car traders also preferred to do business *al fresco*. Back then large groups of them blocked the road in front of their showrooms, their dodgy dealings all in plain sight, but safely out of the earshot of rival villains and the Old Bill. My more legal business took me eastwards to the Inns of Court: Gray's Inn, Lincoln's Inn and The Temple, picking up and dropping off letters and contracts and court documents. If not pressed for time (which I usually wasn't), I would stop at record shops on the way. There was the Virgin Megastore on Tottenham Court Road, the second-hand emporiums in Hanway Street behind it, and little Steve's Sounds in Newport Court down by Chinatown, which offered second-hand nuggets alongside choice new releases in advance of release dates, at prices somehow lower than everywhere else.

With our main office in Portland Place just up the road from BBC Radio's Broadcasting House, there were a couple of notable celebrities I sometimes spotted, who enjoyed living near to their regular place of employment. *Carry On* funny man Kenneth Williams cut a dignified if somewhat wizened and solitary figure in his raincoat, occasionally acknowledging the friendly greetings of other pedestrians on Great Portland Street, as he went back and forth between his Marylebone flat and the Beeb, for his weekly appearance on *Just A Minute*.

In contrast to our beloved Ken (and as if to illustrate all that was to be loathed about the BBC against that which was rightly treasured) was the brazen presence of DJ Jimmy Savile, whose London flat was at Park Crescent, Portland Place, only a few jogs and a suck on his cigar away from our head office.

Unfortunately for us, this local luminary was not easily to be avoided, because he was not just a near neighbour, he was a much valued business associate of the firm we worked for. Jim had fixed it for them to be the architects for the rebuilding of the Stoke Mandeville National Spinal Injuries Unit, his great cause of national renown. The sordid details of how Savile did as he pleased at the Oxfordshire hospital and in the financing and running of its rebuild came out long, long afterwards. Oblivious then to such realities, I was content to sidle past him in the entrance hall as he directed his fake chivalry routine and perverted yodellings towards our star-struck receptionist. I had an inkling he was known to be someone of unconventional appetites, a "dirty old man" even, without having much concern for details. I had never admired Savile, but like most people I thoughtlessly accepted him, on the box and in real life.

The employment agency paid me in cash every week from their office in Villiers Street, and apart from the £50 a month that Mum took for bed and board, my money was my own to play with: records, some clothes, beers, gigs and more gigs. One night at the Electric Ballroom, Platypus managed to almost spoil my evening by blurting out that he and Ant had joined Take It as guitarist and drummer. I was more than somewhat put out. *I* was the one who wanted to join Take It, not them! Happily, my grievance was short-lived; after a rehearsal, both Platypus and Ant decided that the next phase of Igor's unusual project was not for them, so I quickly presented myself to the group's leader and asked for the vacant job. In a short space of time it was all decided: I was Take It's new guitarist, and a lad from Leyton, Dave Morgan, was to be the drummer. We were both invited to move into Igor's house in Hornsey, North London, and my university plans were as dust.

I didn't know Dave, before we moved in. He was a year younger than I, but appeared older, with his big bent nose and gaunt, characterful looks. Like me, he was slender and a tad stoopy, but had more manly granite about him. In those days he didn't bother much with his attire, wearing the same red Wrangler sweatshirt most of the time, but he still looked good. Pretty shy then, a young cockney boy taking all the new stuff in, Dave had a quiet self-assurance which meant he didn't need to talk a lot for people to like him, as we all did. He had already had a job at 16 as a British Rail train driver, which after a life of relative poverty in a large East End family had earned him loads of money. He had spent this lavishly on everything his heart had desired, including a Hornby train set, a Scalextric, some quality power tools and (quite importantly) a drum kit. After the train driving he had been a typewriter engineer, in the course of which he had provided services for the one and only Shakin' Stevens. "Your mate again, Dave," we'd say, whenever the nation's favourite rock'n'roller appeared on *Top Of The Pops*.

The rooms in our old house, let out to us for a trifling £15 a week by Igor's father, had been vacated by Bendle and Nag from The Door & The Window, another of the LMC bands. Boxes of their debut album *Detailed Twang* (NB Records) still lay around the house, left behind in cupboards and under beds. The first pressing of this self-funded record release had sold out to independent record shops and distributors almost immediately, so Bendle and Nag had invested in a second pressing. Unfortunately these had not shifted: those same shops and distributors who took the first pressing were unwilling to buy more of a record that was still occupying space on their shelves.

The Door & The Window aimed to break down the barriers between audience and performer, and at gigs I was usually there at the front to seize any available opportunities for barrier-breaking. At one of their gigs I had gone up on stage with them for their song *Production Line,* along with a few other members of the audience. Protesting at the dehumanisation of factory work, or the soullessness of commercial music-making, or whatever it was, I distinguished myself that night by chanting "*Production line, production line*" with such animated earnestness that I rather stole the show. Later that night, back at the house, Igor mimicked my performance for our amusement.

Igor was a friend, a disciple even, of the revered Green from Scritti Politti. He had sometimes participated in that Camden Town circle of drinkers and thinkers that included Green and Ian Penman, the most hard to understand writer in the *New Musical Express*. Penman briefly had a band called Methodisc Tune, and I had taped their one gig supporting Scritti at the YMCA off Charing Cross Road. Igor lent him my cassette, which the *NME* scribe later flatly refused to return. I thought his band was alright, but I think Penman had a different opinion, and wanted to suppress the evidence. It was a shame, because my tape also had a beautiful version of Scritti's *PAs* on it. Perhaps he wanted that too.

Anyway (a minor digression), their dishevelled Marxist *salon* debated theory, structuralism, post-structuralism, deconstruction, textuality, Barthes, Derrida, Lacan and I knew not what else. Like Green, Igor was frustrated by the confines of the alternative scene we inhabited, and aspired to break out and into mainstream pop. Disruptive entryism was the new praxis. I was all for it. Last week I may have been denouncing bands that had sold out, but this week the merits of unapologetic commercialism laced with subversive messaging had become abundantly clear. Igor had also joined the Labour Party, another entryist project, and I joined too.

The old Take It was no more. Else was gone; only the bass player, Jim Wannell, remained, and a new, proper singer, Etta Saunders, was recruited to replace Igor himself, whose role now was only to write songs and mastermind the whole thing. All was in the service of "The Song", and the plan was to emulate and renew the popular songwriting perfection of the jazz and swing era. Etta adored great jazz singers like Sarah Vaughan and Billie Holiday, and sang in that singerly style.

Igor had good songs. *Private I*, as I understood it, was about public and private identities and constructions of "the true self": *("live in a fiction or die")*. It had a catchy hook and a crafty time signature change that I could never quite master. Another of his compositions, *Criminal,* wedded an appealing, classic-sounding tune with some Robin Hood romanticism and words about breaking the rules of the game.

> *"I don't know why I am this way*
> *Perhaps the answer lies in what I can't say"*

Crime, like pop music, offered a possibility for liberation from the forces of oppression. The idea inspired Igor, Dave and me to plan a Raskolnikov-like robbery of an off-licence in Southgate. We cased the ill-defended establishment, and sized up the proprietor that we would have to intimidate or overpower. We never did it, though; we never named the day. Morgan seemed keen, and with his bony features and east London intonations, he made for a plausible villain. But me? No, not really. I definitely dragged my feet on that one.

I concentrated on learning the fancy chord changes of standards from the American songbook, and hoped to make worthy songwriting contributions of my own. We put together a set, which included Igor's half a dozen songs, an initial offering from me called *Skip It*, and covers like *I've Got My Love To Keep Me Warm* and *I'm Gonna Sit Right Down And Write Myself A Letter*.

In front of a crowd that included The Door & The Window and other friends and well-wishers, we attacked our first gig with great energy and commitment. Our studied approach in rehearsal was usurped on stage by punky, punchy playing and a fair bit of dancing about. We surprised everyone, including ourselves, and we got a great reception and there was much delight. Igor had watched from the side of the stage, and came backstage afterwards, where we enjoyed mutual congratulations. "It Works! It Works!" we said. The buzz was amazing; my first good gig.

We were not the only swingy jazzers in the early 80s pop ferment; the leader in this small field was Vic Godard, managed by The Clash's old manager Bernie Rhodes. Godard fronted the enigmatic Subway Sect, one of the first wave of UK punk bands. Subway Sect's second single, *Ambition* (*"Nothing ever seems to happen to me"*) had been one of the best, but on an indie label and with a less-than-animated stage presence they had not broken into the charts like other punk bands. With more than a little of the Albert Camus about him, Vic was now donning a tuxedo, and his new dalliance with swing was to cement his position as one of the new wave's most resolute outsiders.

Rhodes was showcasing Vic Godard & the Subway Sect at his new Club Left at the Whisky A Go Go in Soho. Subway Sect (Sean McLusky on drums, Chris Bostock on bass, Rob Marche on guitar and Dave Collard on keyboards) were the house band, and Vic, Lady Blue and Dig Wayne were the club singers on alternate weeks. With vaguely Gallic intellectual pretensions, Club Left promised conversation as well as entertainment. Igor urged us all to go, and we did. Maintaining my usual enigmatic silence (in other words, being shy), I don't remember engaging in a lot of conversation, intellectual or otherwise, but I did a lot of dancing. *My Baby Just Cares For Me* by Nina Simone was a Club Left dancefloor favourite, before it became a national hit a few years later. I shuffled around furiously, and came to fancy myself as a fleet-footed hoofer.

I started getting into Fred Astaire and Busby Berkeley musicals, which were sometimes on TV or screened at repertory cinemas like The Scala (then in Tottenham Street, W1), Hampstead's Everyman, and the Electric in Portobello Road. I had been a great frequenter of these places since my earlier teens, to see double and triple bills of films by Woody Allen, the Marx Brothers, Pasolini, Robert Altman, Ken Russell, Kubrick, Peckinpah, all the John Walters trash stuff, zombies and horror. I didn't miss much; I went through most of the art house cinema card. My favourite directors were Nick Roeg (*Performance, The Man Who Fell To Earth*), Roman Polanski (*Rosemary's Baby, Chinatown*) and Martin Scorcese (*Mean Streets, Raging Bull, New York, New York*). Scorcese's *The King of Comedy*, which came out in 1982, spoke to me with a special poignancy.

But what absolutely floored me was the film version of Dennis Potter's *Pennies From Heaven*. Critics had said it wasn't as good as the original BBC TV series, but I thought this movie was the best. Better-cast than the lower-budget TV version, its super-talented stars Steve Martin, Bernadette Peters and Christopher Walken danced and lip-synced to poignant and fantastically-staged musical numbers from the 20s and 30s. Potter's dark, tragic story was told unflinchingly, with the dreamworld of early modern popular entertainment colliding brutally with the harsh realities of the Great Depression – unemployment, pregnancy, poverty and death. The ageing Fred Astaire may have denounced the movie, but I was inspired, and I decided to learn to tap dance. I bought some shoes, joined the Pineapple Dance Centre in Covent Garden and started going to Derek Hartley's weekly jazz tap classes, practising noisily on our kitchen's tiled floor.

Take It progressed, but at no great speed. We wanted to play at Club Left, but the Subway Sect had that all sewn up. Gigs were rare.

I had given up my messenger job to concentrate on music, and was now on the dole like Igor and Dave, but our songwriting output was not prolific. Igor had one new one. I had one too, and one in the pipeline. It was all, perhaps, a little over-deliberated.

We installed, with some Laurel & Hardy-like comic difficulty, my nan's old piano in our basement rehearsal room, and we were doing our best to cajole Igor into playing it, which, happily, he had a talent for. I was particularly keen that he should play in the band, as I knew my weaknesses as a guitar player exposed gaps in our arrangements where soloing and embellishment ought to be. By and by Igor was providing the required tinkly fills, and we also recruited a South African saxophone player called Liduina, and a trumpet player, Barbara Snow.

Young Barbara was quite the pro and had already done a stint working in the fairly famous all-women Ivy Benson Big Band, or what remained of it (she later went on to blow for the Style Council and Jools Holland). A proper English rose, Barbara was full of artless middle-class charm and enthusiasm, and flattered me that I was a good singer. In return, I quietly fell in love with her. Barbara invited me out busking, which she had done before. I was all for it, and suggested I could throw in some tap dancing. "Brilliant idea!" she responded.

So we made our way to South Kensington tube station to give it a go: her with her horn, me in my tap shoes, and a book of jazz standards between us. We hadn't got anything very well worked out. I started singing *All Of Me,* which Barbara punctuated with little improvisations. This had little effect, and the passers-by kept on passing by. But when I started dancing, while Barbara vamped along, the rhythmic tapping turned heads, and coins started coming our way. Before long, the noise we made attracted the attention of a policeman, and we were moved on. We called it a day, but the idea had promise.

South Kensington wasn't a good tube station for busking, but there were a few more established pitches (though equally illegal) in the tunnels at Charing Cross, Oxford Circus, and Green Park tube stations. After some investigation, I persuaded Jim, our bass player, to give it a go with me. He could play some jazzy tunes on electric guitar through my practice amp (he was a much better guitarist than I) and I would confine myself to tap dancing. We practised a couple of things, and then took an early morning train from nearby Hornsey Station to Green Park, to try and get a pitch.

Green Park, with its Mayfair location, was the most lucrative tube station, and had two pitches. These pitches were informally organised into one-hour slots by buskers who passed "the list" of who was due to play from one to the next. Morning slots were best; they paid more, for one thing, and there was less chance your slot would be lost with the list. If a busker was moved on and the pitch left abandoned, another busker was entitled to take it and start another list. On our first effort we got our names on at not too late a time, and it went well, as I remember. We made around £20 in a couple of hours, which after a few goes proved to be roughly what you could expect. This was very acceptable; the cash consisted of coins of all colours (which our local branch of Barclays bank would willingly, almost gratefully, change up for us over the counter) and the odd pound note.

Competition among buskers could be tough; some got night buses to the station to be there when it opened, to win the race for the first pitch. You could get the first train into town from Hornsey at 5.30am, and still find a list extending into the afternoon when you got there. You could put your name down, then go home, have a little sleep, and come out again later in the hope the list was still going. I was willing to do it, I was up for the hunt, but Jim was not so keen.

So I started going down just on my own, dancing to jazz piano tunes played on a Walkman through the practice amp. I randomly combined the steps and rolls I had learnt into improvised routines. It was all in the feet, without much moving about – that was the jazz tap way of doing it, a form of percussion, music as much as dance. Practice was making me faster on my feet, and I soon learned that quicker stepping made faster money. I stuck with bright-tempoed solo piano pieces that swung and left space for me to do my thing. Teddy Wilson's *Sunny Morning* was perfect, and I danced to it over and over again.

When you busk in a tube station you have but a short few moments to impress your audience and get their hands reaching into their pockets, so you show off your most impressive moves, as often as possible, or chances are lost. This is what works, but showing off all the time does tend to fence in your creativity, and it is pretty wearing. This is a general problem with all busking, I think, for musicians as well, especially in subways.

I made as much money on my own as we had as a twosome, and when I tactlessly mentioned this to Jim he bowed out, leaving me to it on my own. I came across as arrogant, I expect, as if I thought our act was all about me. Even if it was, I didn't have to say it. Relations cooled with Jim from then on, and by extension with

Etta, who he was now blissfully shacked up with in the upstairs part of the Take It house.

Others in the house took more kindly to my tap dance antics. Dave and our new buddy Ruth from Swindon spent many a long dole-time hour in our kitchen, drinking tea, smoking, and playing cribbage. But one day they paused this excellent routine of theirs to compose a ditty in my honour, which they typed out on some "Dave Morgan" headed notepaper that his sister had got printed for him. Somehow their tribute, presumably to be sung to the tune of *The Laughing Policeman,* has survived in my possession. A little excerpt:

> *"He gets up every morning*
> *To travel into town*
> *To keep his public happy*
> *He never lets them down*
>
> *Tap tap tap tap tap tap tap*
> *Alan's on the street*
> *Tap tap tap tap tap tap tap*
> *With his dancing feet*
>
> *A man once said to Alan*
> *"I'll help you earn a wage"*
> *He took him off to Hollywood*
> *And put him on the stage"*

And so on it went.

*

Our tastes had changed a lot in a short space of time. But then, there was a big old world of music out there, and I for one had a lot of catching up to do, principally exploring the great kingdoms of jazz, soul, R&B, disco and dance music that up until recently I had paid scarce attention to. Igor had a prized original copy of *The Adventures of Grandmaster Flash on the Wheels of Steel,* and had spotted the commonality of present day rap with the vocal improvisations of King Pleasure and other jazzers from decades before. We listened to these and went on from there, and with a few exceptions most of what we listened to was by black artists.

Rock, as far as I was concerned, was in the bin. Being my simple and over-literal self, I had taken the "Destroy All Rock'n'roll" rhetoric of punk at its word. A little before I stopped buying the weekly rock paper altogether, I had read Paul Morley in the *NME* expanding on Pete Wylie's concept of "rockism"; a new pejorative to bring down rock's tired posturings. But rock against rockism was an oxymoron. In my book, rock had abolished itself. Punk was rock's last hurrah and its final defeat. Rock was history. Rock was a zombie. Rock was *schlock*.

I had stopped tuning in to John Peel and now preferred his old Radio 1 nemesis Tony Blackburn, who had a weekday late-morning soul show on Radio London. Apart from the jazz, swing and American songbook standards we studied (to which I added the songs of Noel Coward, who I rated up there with Cole Porter, the Gershwins and the like), the music we gravitated towards was soul and dance.

We didn't know any soul boys, we barely even knew about them, but we were checking a lot of the same sounds, often championed by Robbie Vincent on his BBC Radio London Saturday show. By '83 my favourite new records were 12" singles. Looking through them now, I pick out *I'm Out Of Your Life* – Arnie's Love, *Get Down Saturday Night* – Oliver Cheatham, *Music* – D Train, *Beat The Street* – Sharon Redd, *Forget Me Nots* – Patrice Rushen, and *A Night To Remember* – Shalamar. Then there were British acts like Shakatak, Freeez, and David Joseph, and we also liked Latin stuff by August Darnell, Tania Maria and Paulinho Da Costa. Added to that, our pot-dealing house visitors Kenny and Tao introduced us to bad boy funkster Rick James; *Standing On The Top* by Rick James & The Temptations, what a great record! We liked James Brown, of course; George Clinton, Parliament, War... all that. We liked The Funk.

Some of our old records we kept and still listened to. My copy of Television's first single, *Little Johnny Jewel* on the Ork label, is a memento of that time. It has a tiny crater on the second side where a little bit of burning blim fell into a groove from one of Morgan's joints. He listened to that record a lot, quite rightly. It still plays; it pops in the instrumental, but it still plays.

A loose alignment of local Crouch End musicians, pot smokers and signers-on gathered with Dave Morgan in our basement to play funky stuff and jam. They ended up calling themselves T-Party. There was John Kettner (lovable bass player, quite eccentric, somewhat posh), Roger Cohen (gifted guitarist, chain-smoking, non-drinking motorist, lived on biscuits), Dave Heley (diminutive, bespectacled, Welsh guitarist, tending to overcompensate by being good at, and right about, nearly everything) and a guy called Cyril (benign, bearded, and in the background). Our friend Nigel Goulding (brother of my future bandmate Dave Goulding) sat in with them on keyboards. Nigel was the first of our mates to have a No. 1 hit, doing that *Full Metal Jacket* mashup with Stanley Kubrick's daughter, Abigail Mead.

Not sure of myself among the musos, I stayed out of all this. I went to dance classes wearing big trousers, braces and leg warmers. I had a baggy sweatshirt with cut-off sleeves and the letters J-A-Z-Z emblazoned on the front of it in the largest possible letters. Sometimes I wore a baseball cap.

My tap dancing busking attracted some media attention. An ITV researcher, Paddy Haycocks, gave me his card at Green Park station and asked me if I would be on the new *Six O'Clock Show*, presented by Danny Baker. Along with a few other buskers I presented myself at the appointed time at a precinct on the South Bank with Igor in tow. He was wearing a piano keyboard tie across which he drew a violin bow up and down, standing by a sign saying, "Give generously, violin required". Like me, Igor would do anything to get on the TV.

Danny Baker appeared. I had reminded myself never to tell anyone, especially the media, how much we buskers earned; that was the buskers' iron rule, enforced by people like Cockney Steve, one of the hardnuts of the Green Park busking fraternity. But when the cheeky TV presenter asked me how much I *really* made, my brain turned to putty and I sang like a canary: "Oh, about 10 pounds an hour" I replied, weakly. Had I been half as mentally quick as I was on my feet, I might have asked him how much *he* made himself; media reports were that the former *Sniffin' Glue* fanzine man was picking up a grand a week for the new show, a fairly astonishing figure then. But that apt riposte goes down as an "if only". Danny then offered me an umbrella, and invited me to do a "singing in the rain" dance around the South Bank; shamelessly I obliged, even though it wasn't raining. After the show went out, I went in to busk the next day fully expecting to be punched by Cockney Steve, but I got away with it.

*

We had looked forward to the new album by Vic Godard & the Subway Sect, *Songs For Sale*, with great anticipation, Igor especially. So much of our hoped-for success depended on theirs: once Vic broke through, we told ourselves, we could follow behind in his slipstream.

But *Songs For Sale* (London Records, 1982) was a complete flop. It was one of those records that you struggled to find in the shops, let alone in the charts. Despite the hiring of hotshot producer Alex Sadkin, the record was disappointingly lightweight, unembellished, and underproduced. And where was *Nice On The Ice*, the song in the live set that we talked of as "the obvious hit", and the "possible Christmas No. 1"? Vic, in a masterstroke of obscurantism, had allowed the album to be released without it, only for a perfectly good version to appear later as a limited edition Benelux import single. The sublime *Stop That Girl,* his previous

Rough Trade single, and still a mainstay of the live set, was another puzzling omission. *Songs For Sale* was a good record, in retrospect, but immensely disappointing at the time. The rest of the Subway Sect had hits with Dig Wayne as JoBoxers, but Vic carried on working as a postman.

We did some recording of our own. Geoff Travis, the top man at Rough Trade, gave us an audience in a back room at their shop, and listened to our first demo, a cover of a swing obscurity called *Tomorrow's Another Day*. He said he liked it, but it was a little "resonant", which was... well... yeah, true. Later, we did a better demo, in a good Denmark Street studio, recorded over two days with a producer friend of Etta's called, if I remember correctly, Floren Florenzu, who did a good job. We recorded a song of Igor's, *I'd Like To Talk To You*, and one of mine, *Fallen Out*. Etta had a liking for red wine; I don't know if she liked my song, which alluded to that fact, but she sang it with me delightfully enough.

> *"Cotes Du Rhone, Beaujolais, whatever comes into my head*
> *True to say... I'd rather drink red than be dead*
> *True to say... I never heard a word you said*
> *True to say... oh! My head!"*

My song had a beginning, an end, a middle eight, and a full set of lyrics that meant something. Well done me. People liked the demo, we liked it, but I'm not sure if any of the right people got to hear it.

We finally got to play at Club Left when it moved to Sunday nights at Ronnie Scott's. It was a big gig for us, a prestigious venue, and it went well, but the swingy pop scene was running out of steam. In the dressing room after the gig, Etta vented her frustrations in my direction and said she didn't want to do it anymore. It was supposed to be *fun*, she said, but we'd taken it all too *seriously*, and it had just got *silly*. I had no response: I just blinked back a little stupidly and felt a little hurt, but Etta had a blossoming career doing something else to take seriously; a serious job earning serious money, so that was that.

> *"It may be a disappointment but*
> *You're not to blame*
> *I cut you up and so you had to cut me out*
> *And tell me that's what life is all about*
> *Passing strangers we laugh at from afar*
> *Passing strangers are exactly who we are*
> *We've fallen out because*
> *I've fallen out of love"*

It was just like the words in my song, you see. Almost, just, like.

*

1984 was drawing near and Igor's dad wanted his house back. Dave and I moved round the corner to the bedsits where Ruth was living, and I set about trying to get us a licensed squat in one of the local short-life housing co-ops. From our window in Church Lane you could see the Kinks recording studio, Konk, on the corner, but I never set foot inside the place, and I never saw a Kink, or any other rock star, go in or out. We did see Pete Astor, though; he lived locally, and we ended up having a good chat with him in Dick's Bar. Just about everyone has a good chat with Pete, if they are fortunate enough to meet him.

Before long Pete had lured Dave away to join his new band, The Living Room. The Living Room became The Loft to distinguish them from Alan McGee's club with the same name, which they were being booked to play at. I went along a few times; Platypus's new band, Twelve Cubic Feet, also played there, also with Dave on drums. They didn't get to be on *Alive In The Living Room,* the live album – and first Creation LP – that documented the club, but The Loft did, and so did I, uncredited, chatting into Leigh Gourney's handheld microphone about Julia & Co between songs. The Loft were soon to put out *Why Does The Rain,* a great single on Creation, and Dave was up and running with a happening band.

I carried on tap dancing. A poster went up in Pineapple, announcing a "national" jazz tap dancing competition to be held at The Canteen (formerly The Blitz, the new romantic mecca). It was going to be judged by American jazz tap legend Will Gaines. I wasn't sure whether to try for the "beginners" or "advanced" competition, but when I started to see who I was up against on the night, young ladies in leotards doing flouncy rhythmless routines, I went all in for the main prize.

When my turn came I walked on and asked the pianist, who hitherto had sat unemployed at the side of the stage, to play something swingy and uptempo, and for two minutes I breezed through some jazz tap improvisations. My dancing teacher, Derek, was watching. He had no idea how I had been putting the steps he had taught me to use, and was aghast. Will Gaines was delighted. I had wiped the floor with the meagre competition, and tapped into victory. Announcing the winner, Will Gaines, slightly embarrassingly, said "It just goes to show... white men really *have* got rhythm!" To which I responded with a nifty *cramp-roll-time-step-heel-toe-STAMP!*

(OK, that last bit I made up; I just stood there, looking immensely pleased with myself.)

Encouraged, I reinvested more of my busking money on further dance classes, not just tap, but the full Arlene Foster jazz dance thing. I set my sights on the West End. I could sing a bit, I could tap dance better than most, so if only I could become a more rounded dancer, I might get a job in a chorus line.

A Chorus Line was the definitive showbiz wannabe musical and a huge hit at the time; if you visited the Pineapple dance studios you could expect to hear the piano intro from *One,* the show's biggest number, coming from one studio or another. Barbara had the album and I grew to love it; the 70s Marvin Hamlisch score was great, and the book captured the narcissism of show people in all their neurotic glory.

The trouble was, I wasn't that good a dancer. I could tap, but my talent was all in my feet. I had none of the suppleness and athleticism that professional dancing demanded. I was barely able to touch my toes without bending my knees, let alone anything else. And speaking of knees, these and my ankles were aching and breaking down from pounding those solid tube station stones. Dancers need sprung wooden floors, and I was doing myself an injury. I was now managing only one hour of busking a day.

The only way was down. I was introduced to a fringe theatre chap called Eric who was (supposedly) putting a mixed theatre production together for the Edinburgh Fringe Festival. It featured Twelve Cubic Feet, a poet friend of ours called Duncan who lived on tinned fish and heroin, Eric himself, and a few others. What was the show going to be? It was all very vague. I asked Eric when we were going to rehearse, but we never did. What did he want me to do? He assured me not to worry, and to leave it to him.

We made it up to Edinburgh, despite going in very overloaded cars, but our show was a farce, and not the funny kind. It consisted of nothing more than each of us doing our party pieces in succession, and the band doing their set. Before I came on, Eric had done a mime which involved bursting balloons, which hadn't worked because one of the balloons had already burst, just as he went on. He went through the charade of continuing his bit, pretending that the burst balloon was still inflated. Ridiculous.

I then took the stage, in my tap-dancing get-up, to do an unaccompanied routine. Or maybe I danced while Twelve Cubic Feet did their set, I can't remember. All I can remember was the audience: two paying customers and the theatre critic from *The Scotsman*, sitting there, looking at me.

The following night, thank goodness, the show was pulled. No matter. We were in Edinburgh, staying in free and comfy student accommodation. The weather was fine, and there were endless good shows to go and see throughout the day, with tickets less than a pound. It was a great festival, back then. I saw some memorable performances – contemporary dance, funny poets, a Berkoff play, comedians, Eric Bogosian's *Talk Radio* solo show – and when the money had almost run out, there was still the student bar disco where we danced ecstatically to New Order's *Blue Monday* every night, on cheap beer and no drugs whatsoever.

After this, I greeted offers of work with greater scepticism. A sexy young lass from Cheshire came up to me and said she could get me a summer season on a Greek island holiday complex. She thought my tap dancing would combine well with a nubile young contortionist she was working with. I was not persuaded.

John Walters, John Peel's affable producer, saw me tapping on the tube and invited me on his show. It was a new "non-music" magazine show he had on BBC Radio, called *Walters' Weekly*. I went up to the office he shared with Peely at Portland Place, which was decorated with years of Christmas cards that, Miss Havisham-like, they never took down. Then we went down to the George on Great Portland Street to enjoy afternoon beers with cast members of *The Archers*, and after that we contrived an on-location interview in a tunnel at Charing Cross station. I announced to him that I was planning a new group, The Gold Diggers Of 1984. John was bluntly uninterested. "Everyone's got a band," he said, and asked me something about tap dancing.

He had a point. In our world, everyone was in a bloody band, or wanted to be. He was bored with it all, and maybe I was too. Maybe I needed to move on and see another side of life. It was time for a hiatus. It was time to give the pop a rest.

A Brief Prehistory Of The Rockingbirds

BY THE END of 1987 two important things had happened for me. One was I now had a philosophy degree, and the other (more importantly) was I had learned to love country music.

I had gone to North London Polytechnic (or the Polytechnic of North London, if you prefer). PNL had the worst job placement record in the country, and my course had the worst job placement record in the college. Well... so somebody told me, I wasn't sure if it was true, and I didn't care all that much if it was. I was just there to study something interesting, have a good time if I could, and get paid for that privilege, as you could in those happy days, courtesy of a student grant, fees all paid.

I had been successful in my quest to get cheap housing for me, Dave and Ruth through a short-life housing co-operative in Haringey. The deal was, you could get a room in a shared house belonging to the council or a local housing association, on condition you vacated it when the owner wanted it back. It was squatting with a licence, and you paid the co-op a £6 a week licence fee (rent, in other words) which funded boilers, plumbing, rewiring, heaters or anything else that might make life in your substandard property more comfortable. It was a good idea, and there were lots of such local co-ops, who negotiated with the housing providers through their umbrella group, Haringey Short Life Users (HSLU).

The Noel Park Housing Co-operative management committee met weekly in Brabant Road Trade Union Centre in Wood Green. If you wanted to be housed by Noel Park, you had to go along to the meeting to get on the waiting list, or, if that was full, on the waiting list for the waiting list; then you had to attend as many meetings as you could, to demonstrate your "co-operability". I had no difficulty making that weekly commitment, especially in a trade union subsidised bar, and as a Labour Party member, now secretary of the local Young Socialists, I was an experienced meeting-goer who went to the same hall for local party gatherings. Within the space of a year I had graduated from being a non-member on the Noel Park Housing Co-operative waiting list, to housed member paying £6 a week, and then to elected committee member and officer, living rent-free.

The business of the co-op committee meetings included collecting rent from members on the night, dealing with those who didn't pay, allocations, drinking, and squabbling. The two co-op factions were an older guard of members who liked to run things to suit themselves, and newer people like me ("fascist bureaucrats" as we were once described) who felt a few things could improve and be done correctly.

It was surprising how many people didn't pay their rent, considering it was almost nothing. Maybe that was it; the cost was so little, people tended to think they could pay it any time, so their arrears drifted upwards towards £100 and over and, before they knew it, they were in trouble. Dave Morgan was terrible at paying his rent, and we had to give him an NTQ – a 'notice to quit' letter. He did a runner and moved into a rented flat with his girlfriend, Phoebe Flint. They could afford it because his new band with Pete Astor, The Weather Prophets, had just got a deal on Alan McGee's major-backed Elevation label. Morgan was in the money.

International singing star Sade and her man-about-town partner Robert Elms were two other naughty non-payers we had to resort to law to boot out, though we knew they had already departed and given their keys to some friends. Surreal comedian Kevin McAleer was another notable resident; we had seen him at the Sunday night alternative comedy night at Brabant Road. He was hilarious, *and* paid his rent.

The old Noel Park council estate, where we had most of our houses, nestled to the east side of the newly-built Wood Green Shopping City. The poet Stevie Smith had written of "the dark chimneys of Noel Park", but under those grey slate roofs there now lurked a darker, sinister secret. I had heard talk of IRA cells in the co-op and Kalashnikovs under floorboards. There were certainly IRA sympathisers about; among these were a few of my comrades in the Young Socialists who were part of the Socialist Organiser newspaper group which had future Labour leader Jeremy Corbyn MP among their number. One of them, I remember, lived on Noel Park in another co-op. He hero-worshipped Gerry Adams, and had proudly shown us a photograph of himself with the Sinn Féin leader, taken at a conference on Palestine that he had attended as our delegate.

But real terrorists? I did not give it much credence, but it proved to be true. One night in 1988 the anti-terrorist squad sealed off Bury Road and found arms and explosives in one of our houses. Eamon, a fellow committee member, was arrested with his housemate Nick Mullen, who had been running the Brabant Road bar. Eamon was eventually released, but Mullen got 30 years for conspiracy to cause explosions. This saved us the trouble of evicting *him* for not paying his rent.

My housemates and I had not lived on the Noel Park estate proper. Our first house was in Cobham Road, near Turnpike Lane tube. When that house went back, the co-op acquired 1, Palace Road in Bounds Green for us from a housing association, Circle 33. T-Party guitarist Dave Heley, who had moved into Cobham Road after Dave had done his flit, came with, and Ruth had her builder boyfriend from Swindon staying over a lot of the time.

Heley had made vegetarians out of all of us who were not ones already. On his arrival at Cobham Road he rustled up a tasty meat-free meal for everybody, we reciprocated in kind the next day and a daily communal meal became a regular thing. Friends had a habit of turning up early in the evening when we were likely to be serving up; John and Roger from T-Party, for instance. It was a nice scene; some wine would come from somewhere, and something to smoke. Phoebe was around a lot, especially when Morgan was away touring. Then he fell for someone else on his travels, he and Phoebe split up, and she was around even more. Phoebe sang with T-Party. Her dad, drummer Hughie Flint, was in The Blues Band, and had been fifty per cent of McGuinness Flint.

Our new abode, destined to be demolished, was built on a railway siding and was subsiding towards the tracks below. An upstairs back room had a crack in the wall you could see daylight through. Below was a collapsing glass conservatory which, should you hazard to go in, had a fine selection of old-style terracotta flower pots of all sizes and some rusty hand-made woodworking and gardening tools that I imagined had been the previous occupant's pride and joy. I had a go at gardening, but the bindweed from the adjacent wasteland strangled everything. It was a nice place for a cat though, and we got a little tabby that we called Funk (because, as I mentioned before, we liked the funk). Heley renamed her Skunk, which was more fitting.

So I was already well ensconced in North London with my own set of friends, and I wasn't depending on North London Poly to provide me with a lot of new ones. But I made two good friends in the first year, who made a big difference to me.

Malcolm was the first person I spoke to in the Kentish Town student bar. We connected because he knew the T-Party guys; he had been a blues guitarist, and was known on the London blues jam scene that they sometimes participated in. Obsessed with Robert Johnson, Malcolm had learned to play all the songs on *King Of The Delta Blues Singers*. John and Roger confirmed that he could play all that stuff exactly as on the record, a remarkable mimetic feat. But after conquering Robert Johnson, Malcolm's interest in playing music had declined, and he had done a year of A-level logic before starting our philosophy course. My story was a little similar, having quit music to do the same. We went on from there, instant best friends, remaining that way through the next three years. I always think of Malcolm in Levi jeans, Dunlop Green Flash plimsolls and a collarless shirt, often with an untucked tail sticking out from under his blazer. About the same age as me but with hair thinning prematurely, he was not a big lad; light enough for me to dangle him by his ankles over the side of a ferry one boozy morning on a camping trip to Amsterdam.

During long drinking and smoking sessions in the student bar and other haunts, Malcolm would often deep-dive his latest philosophical investigations with me there for a sounding board, but his reasonings would soon soar off beyond my understanding. The best I can say to characterise his thinking is that he combined rigorous logic (his essays containing arguments presented in logical formulae) with a devotion to Sartre. He was obsessed by *Nausea* (the novel and the concept) and knew passages from the impenetrable existentialist opus *Being And Nothingness* by heart.

It seemed Malcolm had come to college knowing nearly all there was to know of his subject in advance. Perhaps that's why he came to lowly PNL, it didn't really matter what college he went to; he was, in essence, an autodidact, and this was just a stepping stone to where he wanted to go. He ran rings around most of our tutors, who he dismissed with disdain, and mimicked with amusing inaccuracy when he was very pissed.

Academically I settled comfortably enough in Malcolm's shadow. I applied myself, sporadically, and got good marks for some of my essays. I was genuinely interested in the subject, but I have never been bookish or well-read. Of our primary texts I read only the mercifully short Descartes' *Meditations* and Kant's *Grundlegung* in their entirety. For the rest, I picked up the broad concepts you needed for philosophical speculation from lectures and secondary texts like Flew's *Dictionary Of Philosophy,* which I enjoyed flicking through in much the same way I had enjoyed my *NME Book Of Rock*. Philosophy had become my new frontier of fascination.

Academic life in the first term of our first year was overshadowed by political agitations that put our college in the news. Patrick Harrington was a philosophy student like ourselves, in his third and final year. He was also an active party member of the anti-immigration National Front, and the Socialist Worker Party-dominated student union mounted a campaign to have him thrown out, in defence of black and Asian students at the college.

An occupation of the building in protest at Harrington's presence was planned, and Malcolm and I debated whether to join in. It was an issue I had encountered at my very first Labour Party ward meeting in Crouch End, when Councillor Toby Harris had taken flak for allowing the NF to book a local hall. I was a waverer on the ethical chestnut of what should be permissible in thought and word. That time, I had voted with my activist friends for an NF ban, despite being privately more sympathetic with Harris's arguments and legal predicament. This time, I had Malcolm to sway me; what had Patrick Harrington actually done, other than voice a political opinion? Malcolm was doubtful, he wanted to get on with his work, and when he was not being unintelligible, Malcolm was usually persuasive.

It proved, however, that he was not as sure on the matter as he had seemed. I stayed home during the week of the occupation, oblivious to all that was going on, but on my return I found Malcolm had thrown himself wholeheartedly into the anarchic fun of the protest, enjoying boozy all-night revels, go-fast drugs, nightly video screenings of *The Blues Brothers*, and whatever other bonding activities had gone on among the fresher participants that I had unwittingly denied myself.

Whatever the noble intentions, it is the power of the group and the urge to belong that usually prevails. Malcolm perhaps felt it more than I did, but I did too, and, playing catch-up, I supported subsequent protests. When the word went round that Harrington had gone into the library one morning, students followed in, myself included, to non-violently torment the man. With all our eyes upon him, the tall, tie-wearing neo-nationalist went through a charade of browsing the Ethics section, opening one book, and then studiously eyeing another. Our fellow philosopher and future historian Paul Lay came and stood close at his shoulder, opening books at random in mockery of his perusals. Respecting the quiet sanctity of the library, we indulged in no anti-fascist chanting as this went on. Instead, a spooky-voiced whisper went up, "Patrick, we want you... OUT!", which gradually increased in its menacing emphasis with each repetition, with some of us adding the word "DEAD" in place of "OUT" as our target made his way towards the library desk, to check out John Stuart Mill (or whatever it was he was borrowing).

Eventually Harrington won a court order to prevent further protests and pickets. Students who defied this were threatened with prison, and lecturers who refused to name names also felt the heat. A compromise was reached where Harrington was to be given off-site tutoring to keep him away from campus, and then Christmas came.

Early in the new year, I was walking up Kentish Town High Road towards the tube station when the familiar figure of Patrick Harrington came striding past. Stopping outside the Owl Bookshop, I did a quick double take, turned around, and followed as he marched towards the Prince of Wales Road college building and tripped up the steps and through the front door as if the events of last term had never happened. Dashing into the student union office with some urgency, I alerted whoever was there that the enemy was once again in our midst. My news was met with indifference, and a modicum of embarrassment not so much on their part as for me, so woefully off-message. The campaign to eject Patrick Harrington was over; last term's thing. We had wanted him out. We had wanted him DEAD. He was still here.

As with most situations in life, at college I tended to be part there, and part somewhere else. Malcolm was earnestly absorbed in his work, but was still funny and a good mixer, whereas I, though often in his presence, went mostly unnoticed. He must have seen something in me, so I supposed, and we had a few larks, one of which, a singular and, I think, salient little tale, I shall now relate.

Early in our first summer break Malcolm had found a job laying a lawn for Prof. Fred Halliday. The professor was a prominent expert on the Middle East, and was sometimes interviewed in that capacity on the news. He lived in Cranley Gardens, at the foot of Muswell Hill, which had also been in the news, in times quite recent, as the crime scene locale of the serial killer Dennis Nilsen, who had picked up his lonely male victims in the nearby pubs.

Admiring Malcolm's lawn-laying work over the garden fence, Fred Halliday's neighbours, also academics who had a couple of teenage daughters, asked him if he would mind doing a few jobs for them: some clearance work and the building of a small wall, nothing grand. Malcolm said he could if he could bring a helper along (me) because it was a double-handed job. An hourly rate was agreed, cash to be paid on the day. They liked that we were students and academics like them, and they liked that we would be cheap.

Our first visit went well enough. Concrete, sand and bricks had been delivered. We cleared the area, dug a decent trench where the wall was to be, vigorously mixed the concrete, filled the trench and levelled it off. For our evident sweat and toil in the sun we were rewarded with cheese salad baguettes, a cold can of Heineken lager each, and cash at the end of the day. So far, so OK.

But the next day, we were to lay the bricks on the foundation. I asked Malcolm if he'd laid bricks before and he said he had not. Neither had I. We had a spirit level, though; it would be fine, he reassured me. I had brought along some string, believing this was required according to the accepted technique for the laying of bricks. Malcolm brushed this technical nicety aside; we could keep the wall straight by using the edge of the spirit level, and what wasn't laid straight could easily be repositioned and righted. In a few hours we had a small wall. It wasn't very straight, but it was deemed adequate to its purpose, which was to mark the boundary of a previously ill-defined terrace at the side of the house, one of two terraced steps that went down to the lawn.

Our employer (it might have been him, it was probably her) thought for a moment. Perhaps a somewhat larger wall could be placed alongside the flowerbeds in front of the fence? What did we think about that? Certainly, said Malcolm. And so began a succession of piecemeal additions that gradually grew over the following days and weeks into a monstrosity of irregularly-constructed and ill-planned improvisations, occasionally but never confidently referred to as a "patio", that was built with the most expensive handmade bricks and the cheapest, crumbliest flagstones, by two entirely unqualified workmen.

From the earliest stage I was ill at ease with what we were constructing, and my anxiety and guilt grew in proportion to its size and crookedness. Admittedly, if you looked at it from the end of the garden and squinted your eyes it perhaps looked alright, but if you looked closer, from any aspect, the irregular lines, angles, overhangs and juttings-out were numerous and plain to see. I tried to raise my anxieties with Malcolm when I met him at his place on the way up to the house. Malcolm was dismissive and told me not to worry about it. Then he would roll a big joint, give me a couple of puffs to intensify my feelings of paranoia, and off we set again. He was sublimely unconcerned – as, for the most part it seemed, were they.

Each morning as we walked up that hill to the house to get to work, I was filled with foreboding, and was convinced that this time, after that *ridiculous* thing we did yesterday, the scales must surely fall from their eyes and they would see our shoddy work for what it was. He would sometimes hazard little criticisms, and question the direction and cost of the project, but his wife would hear none of it, and take any fault-finding as criticisms of her. There was a tension there, and we sometimes heard their muted bickering as we worked, which once rose to her crying out "Oh, *Mark!*" before their embarrassing conference was abruptly terminated. He always relented, and she always prevailed. The suppressed recriminations and tears that I expected to burst forth each day never materialised. Each morning we would arrive at their front door, with me expecting this to be the last time, and each time she would answer with a cheery jingle of the side-door keys, to let us back into the garden to add to the atrocity.

The work continued through the summer, and like Zeno's arrow, the project moved towards its end, without any prospect of that end ever being reached. It was only when term-time approached that we were relieved of our duties, only out of consideration to *us*, we were reassured, so we could concentrate on our education, which was *the* most important thing. They could get somebody in to finish off the job, they said. Presumably it was left to some competent working artisan to mock their folly to their faces before demolishing all we had done.

The whole absurd saga resembled a Mike Leigh movie satirising middle-class academics, with me somehow in the middle of it. It was also a pointed case study in practical philosophy, exactly of the epistemological kind we did at college. Assuming our sensory data to be more or less the same, how can people look at identical things and perceive and understand them so very differently? It is a question I have wondered about at various points in my life, and never more so than in recent years, as I have found myself increasingly at odds with people around me. I am now inclined to think the educated can be the most resistant to seeing and accepting what is in front of them, if the realities that present themselves disagree with what they want to see, or what their education has taught them to expect.

My other college buddy was Myles. Myles was a 30-something Irishman with a French-sounding surname. Like Malcolm, Myles had come to college with little to learn from his tutors. He was extremely well-read and familiar with the canonical figures of literature and philosophy. Like me he was really just looking for something to do and somewhere to go, but Myles did not last long at college, only a term or so. His first essay, on John Locke's primary and secondary qualities, was well over 25 pages long, written out beautifully in longhand with his favoured fine Tempo fibre tip. His tutor returned it to him, unread and unmarked. Too long, he said. Myles was indignant. Quite unable to conform with the strictures of the course, he left.

But we stayed in touch. He lived near me in a Wood Green bedsit, liked a drink, and knew stuff. Myles was a nervous kind of guy; slight, bespectacled, and a chain-smoker of cheap Dunhill Superkings. He had been in a bad motorcycle accident some years before, and now lived with the after-effects of his injuries: impaired mobility and physical and mental pain.

Myles had also been a musician, back in the 70s. He had played fingerpicking folk/country guitar, and had been a bassist in a touring showband, which was a big thing in Ireland, back then. He had known the Miami Showband, the most famous of all of those groups, famous for being massacred in Northern Ireland by the loyalist UVF paramilitary in 1975. Myles had later gone to West Germany to work on one of the US Army bases as some kind of entertainments manager. Those bases had big budgets to attract major acts to come and play, and Myles booked a lot of American country singers. He also booked The Dubliners, generously meeting their outrageous rider demands for Guinness and Irish whiskey, before, during and after their shows. Impressed by his recollections of their prodigious alcohol consumption, I was unwise enough to try to emulate such exploits with my own band, as will be seen.

My friend's small bedsit was full of books and records. One whole wardrobe he had stacked full of contemporary crime novels, recently acquired and read. A crime novel is a great window into the social environment of the day, Myles told me. Most of the books he had owned and read were lost, destroyed; he had left them in a friend's leaking outhouse in Germany. All his remaining books had his neat and methodical notes and markings, made with that trademark Tempo pen. I used to enjoy reading his old Dostoyevskys with the help of these notes, though sometimes his underlinings extending across whole paragraphs and pages were a tad over-emphatic.

Myles encouraged me to listen to country music, a genre I had previously dismissed as shallow and uninteresting. He made me a tape with songs by John Prine, Guy Clark, Emmylou Harris, David Blue, Nanci Griffith, Kris Kristofferson, Kinky Friedman and Willie Nelson, all names I had little knowledge of. He had a copy of Gram Parsons' *Grievous Angel* in pride of place among his records. I thought the dreamy blue cover looked bland and uninteresting, not my kind of thing, but Myles was insistent this was the stuff: cosmic American country music. The album's signature track, *The Return Of The Grievous Angel*, was on my cassette, and this strange, meandering, chorus-less road movie of a song has been on many a setlist of mine ever since, taking me down 20,000 country roads of saloon bars, billboards, truck stops and Bible Belt desert and prairie with a king in an amphetamine crown met along the way.

Elvis Presley, The King himself, was a big bridge for me into country music. I had not been a great fan up until then; he didn't write his own songs, for one thing, and although I had liked *Heartbreak Hotel* and a few other songs as a kid, I had come to see him as a sad exemplar of backward white conservatism, a pre-punk dinosaur who had allowed Las Vegas cabaret trappings, ugly obesity and deadly prescription drugs to consume his talent.

But there was a guy at college, Mark – Black Mark people called him, being as he was – who was an Elvis fan. I went to a party where Mark DJ'ed and got everyone dancing to his Elvis 45s, and had a glorious epiphany: Elvis truly was the King. I bought *The Sun Sessions* and learned to strum the songs, just like the singer on the record, on my left-handed Eko Ranger acoustic guitar. Before long my housemates and friends were hooked on the King as well, and our dilapidated Bounds Green house became home to an Elvis-adoring cult. Many a late morning the "Uh-huh huh..." vocal intro to *Good Luck Charm* would come bursting forth from Heley's bedroom, like a Reveille to rouse the King's company from their dreamy pits, to start our day as we intended to go on. We played mostly Elvis for months on end, and I was born again.

Through Elvis I discovered his close 50s contemporaries. Sun Records compilations led to Roy Orbison, Jerry Lee Lewis, and Johnny Cash. Famous names, of course, but I listened now, as to Elvis, with fresh and receptive ears. I was impressed at how simple, how primal, so much of it was, how so much could be done with just a few chords. This was a more direct route to successful songwriting than the jazzier structures I had toyed with a few years before. From these inspirations, I was one step away from my last key discovery, Hank Williams.

Like Elvis, Hank Williams was a poor white and ignorant hillbilly, touched with divinity. His voice spoke with colloquial Southern simplicity, sang with the pain of all humanity, and haunted like a ghost. The songs he sang were sometimes complicated (for instance, *Lovesick Blues)*, usually not, but always direct and timeless. Tune-wise, there is little to distinguish the simple three-chord bop of Hank's hit *Move It On Over* from Bill Haley's *Rock Around The Clock* or any number of Marc Bolan's boogies; they all tapped into the same marvellous muse. Also like Elvis, Hank had a magnetism and a tragic charisma, but while Elvis was all youthful vigour and promise before his fall, Hank, with his painful spinal defect and piercing, runty look, had tragedy baked in from the start.

Elvis and Hank had opened up a great new vista for me. Country music required talent and musicianship, like any other, but its fundamentals were accessible and universal. Though my scorn for most things rock would remain, country music opened up a new and genuine possibility, and country rock I was to allow as an exception. I had an inkling that with heart, commitment and a modicum of wit, an English pretender like me might be able to do something with it.

But any fresh stirrings I had in a musical direction were on hold while I attended to the immediate need for paid employment, once my three years at college had come to an end. The Polytechnic of North London had left me ill-prepared for the world of work. A talk about TEFL (teaching English as a foreign language), given by the head of our course, was the only guidance I remember them offering, and it had struck me at the time as a blunt indication of the low expectations they had for us. Even I could deduce that the English teaching foreign legion was the career option of last resort, the miserable preserve of social misfits, oddballs and (so it would seem) PNL philosophy graduates.

It was 24th December, 1987, Christmas Eve, and Myles and I had gone out for a drink. We'd been talking about an idea of his to start a literary research business together, a kind of detective agency for writers. There were a couple of such concerns listed in the *Writers' & Artists' Yearbook*. There was no knowing whether such enterprises prospered, but it was an intriguing idea. Walking back to his bedsit after the pub, and feeling sad about him being on his own at Christmas, I asked him if he'd like to come and spend the next day with us Tylers. Myles didn't celebrate Christmas, but he agreed to come.

It all went badly. I knew he would find my family setting unfamiliar, but assumed he would make some kind of festive effort: I was wrong. My friend remained tight-lipped and ill-at-ease throughout the day, refusing to offer up anything more than the briefest replies to our polite enquiries, and occasionally casting his eyes from side to side, like a confined animal looking for a way to escape. In the evening we visited in-laws. Drinks were downed, but an attempt at a game of Pictionary only heightened Myles'(and my) anxiety. Then my father decided to introduce a note of seriousness into proceedings, and asked me that dreaded but inevitable question: "So... Alan, what are you going to *do* with yourself, now you have finished college?" Armed with nothing else by way of a reply, I foolishly resorted to honesty and opened up about the writers' research idea Myles and I had been considering. I may have hoped that introducing the subject would tease out some conversation from my embarrassingly petrified guest, but pressed by my dad and others for more details about our enterprise, Myles shut up like a clam. Mortified, no doubt, by my indiscretion, he never once mentioned his business idea to me again.

After college, Malcolm walked into a job at the University of Leeds, buying a house in Hunslet nearby, and after that he went on to teach philosophy at York. I presumed he was destined to be a major academic figure, a Bertrand Russell for the 21st century, but it was not to be. By the mid-90s, absorbed in my own shenanigans, I lost touch with both Malcolm and Myles. I don't know what became of either of them, efforts to find them since have come to nought, and for that reason I haven't given their full names. They were good friends though, and I have missed them.

*

My initial idea after college was not to start a new band of my own: it was to join one, as a drummer. I had been envious of Dave Morgan's progress up the indie rock ladder with The Loft and The Weather Prophets. I coveted the attention he had received, the tours, the tall tales and the lump sums of cash more considerable than the student grants that had come my way. Decent drummers, I knew, were always in demand. I had rhythm, as the tap dance king Will Gaines had confirmed. Tap dancing was my one acknowledged talent, and I hoped that whatever made me good at that would enable me to master a full drum kit.

But it was not to be. I installed a kit in the upstairs back room with its big crack in the wall, and practised diligently, for a few months, only to have it confirmed once again that my talent was principally located below my knees. I was okay with the paradiddle and mummy/daddy drum exercises that Dave showed me, but when I tried to coordinate these with hands and feet together, my body gradually tensed like a coiled spring till I broke down like a wind-up toy.

So there was nothing else for it. If my destiny was in music (which was the best thing my imagination could conceive for myself), I would have to write my own songs, some country songs, and get a band together to play them.

I began with a guy from college who had once wanted to start a band playing trucking songs, but he had got himself a job and was no longer interested. No matter, there were people much closer to home. Stan Patrzalek was another old Swindon friend of Ruth's who was now in my gang on the housing co-op committee. He had a Butthole Surfers-type group who rehearsed their loud electric racket standing on plastic crates above great pools of water in his waterlogged basement on Westbury Avenue. Despite this disregard for health, safety *and* taste, Stan and I had plenty in common; he was part of our Elvis fandom, and he was up for trying bass. Phoebe was also game. We could double up on vocals, like Ellie Marshall and Jonathan Richman on *Rockin' And Romance,* a record she loved as I did.

We three got together for a play in the back room. The bass was the only thing amplified. I wasn't bothering with microphones, as Jonathan Richman could manage without and we believed in belting the songs out with a "full voiced" approach. Once started, Heley walked in, uninvited but very welcome, and with my drum kit sitting there unused, he started playing them in earnest for the first time in his life, a job the quick-witted guitarist took to more easily than I had. We had a band, and I already had a name for us: The Rockingbirds.

These prehistoric Rockingbirds were not to do many gigs. Our first was at the old boxing club in Highgate, in the middle of the roundabout on the A1, supporting T-Party. We did just four songs, *Standing At The Doorstep Of Love, Living In A Trailer, You're The Kind Of Boy,* and a song by Phoebe, *You'll Be Back.* I invited my new girlfriend along, a first night out. Experience tells me that turning your own gig into a date is never a great idea, but on this one occasion, it worked. Chloe was very impressed, which was all the praise and reassurance a chap like me was looking for.

With most of us not playing our first-choice instruments, and with my limited guitar craft, our sound may have had a raw appeal, but I knew we needed some Scotty Moore-like guitar magic to enliven our arrangements. We turned to Piece.

THE WEATHER PROPHETS

Piece Thompson was a few years older than us. He had been the latter-day guitarist for The Weather Prophets, who had recently called time after their second album, with Pete Astor now going solo. In a Creation Records publicity photo – the only picture I could find with Piece in the band – he appears in a pinstripe jacket, gazing off a little ruefully betwixt Pete on the left and the two shades-wearing Daves. Brought in as a replacement for Oisin Little,

Piece was a touring member of The Weather Prophets but (to my knowledge) never made a record with them. He had previously enjoyed a more prominent role with Turkey Bones & The Wild Dogs, an anarchic combo from his hometown of Perth, Scotland, who once made the front cover of *Sounds*. He got his nickname at school from the "jammy piece" (bread and jam sandwich) his impoverished mother always made him for his lunch. His real name was Colin, and after school he had worked as a gas fitter, before bringing his left-handed Fender Telecaster to London. Like a few Scots I've known, he liked to exaggerate rather than tone down his Scottish brogue for the English listener.

Piece had a reputation for being somewhat mercurial, a bit of an awkward customer, "an offy man" even, to use one of his own favourite colloquialisms. Undeterred, I went to see him at his neat little flat in King's Cross. After a few beers in the King Charles pub next door, we went back to his with some take away tinnies to listen to albums by The Replacements and World Party that he had bought that week. Piece was cagey and wasn't sure if he was the man for us. "I'm no really a lead guitarist," he protested, "I just wannae play rhythm and stay in the background." But I had seen and heard him on his battered Tele and was convinced he had something there that would make all the difference for us.

I don't remember the band rehearsing with Piece, and I don't think we ever did a gig. A demo recording was planned, at Vons in Liverpool Road, Islington. Vons did a cheap all-nighter deal, and Piece knew one of the guys there. I booked two separate nights. On the first, the rest of us – Dave, Stan, Phoebe and I – put the basic tracks down. Piece was then given a rough mix on cassette so he could work out what he was going to play at the next visit, which Piece bigged up with wide-eyed, semi-piss-taking relish as "The Night Of The Guitars".

When our much-vaunted "Night of the Guitars" came, excitement got the better of us. I had brought a quantity of whiskey, but it would have been better had I bought a guitar tuner, as my soon-sozzled guitar wizard struggled to get his axe in tune. Interminable and increasingly unsuccessful attempts at tuning continued into the wee hours of the morning, driving me, he and our engineer half-mad.

At some point an approximation of being in tune must have been reached, the final recording being the proof of it. The demo was... good, dammit! Listening back now, *Lucky Lonesome Smile* was an uplifting pop tune with nicely-layered guitars, and *Standing At The Doorstep Of Love* had a stronger country vibe that fired along plaintively and made its point. Some of Stan's trendy friends in Islington were given a tape, and he said they really liked what we'd done. Had we put *Lucky Lonesome* out as a single, it might have made an impression on the indie charts. But I never properly considered that option; it was only a demo, I thought, and I wasn't sure what to do next.

*

Things were afoot in the world of Haringey short-life housing co-ops. The council was giving us grief for not being "equal ops" enough and allocating housing to our friends. The fact that the housing we got from the council had been deemed unfit to be let and was only acceptable to punks, hippies and doleys like us was glossed over. The bigger picture, though, was they didn't have empty houses to licence out like they used to, and wanted all their remaining stock back. In compensation, a plan was devised to decant us into "hard to let" council tenancies in less-desirable parts of London, like yet-to-be gentrified Hackney, and boroughs south of the river. There were a few complaints about the loss of our community, but most of us did very well out of the deal: permanent housing, social rents, and rights to buy on the cheap, courtesy of Maggie Thatcher's popular giveaway government.

But I wasn't to be one of these. I passed on getting a council flat for a more interesting option. My co-op friend Deborah, who now managed a small housing association, had a large property in Camden that they had acquired; would I take occupancy of it, rent-free, and be responsible for looking after it so it could be returned to them when they asked? My answer was yes, yes, and very emphatically *yes*. NW1 was a much more exciting postcode to have as an address than E5 or SE8. Taking Dave Morgan with me, who had been languishing somewhat since the breakup of The Weather Prophets, I parked us smack dab in the centre of the London indie music scene: Camden Town.

Cowboys in Camden Town

THE HOUSE WAS a short walk away from the Falcon, probably Camden's most popular small venue, with gigs nearly every night. Most British bands covered by the music papers would have played the Falcon; Suede played there, Blur got signed there, and it was where Lush, who I recognised from my time at North London Poly in Kentish Town, did their first gig. The Falcon was where the shoegazers played (Chapterhouse, Slowdive, Swervedriver), and where the Camden Lurch scene began (Silverfish, Th' Faith Healers, Skyscraper). It was also home ground to numerous outlier bands like Gallon Drunk, Hippies With Muscles, and, before long, ourselves. Many of these bands and their friends and hangers-on formed the pub's nightly clientele.

The Falcon was owned by Baxter, an aloof Scotsman who left the running of the pub to the appalling Graham. During the day, Graham ran a used tyre business that he directed from various public houses along the route from his council flat in Hampstead to the pub he managed in the evening. According to Graham, his business was prosperous, and he bragged to us about how he had bought his wife the most expensive steam iron in her mail order catalogue. He was a complete alcoholic, and once lifted up his shirt to reveal the bruising on his abdomen caused by excessive beer consumption. He had only six months to live, so he said, and didn't seem to care, making it difficult for the rest of us to care either. Graham was never pleasant, but he saved his worst for the end of the evening, when he bawled at his customers to "finish yer fuckin' drinks, get out of my fuckin' pub, take yer fuckin' girlfriend home, and FUCK HER!" I remember the ashen faces of my mother, father and sister when I unwisely invited them to one of our gigs there.

The venue was in the back room, a compact, well-proportioned gig space with a decent enough stage. A little before my time it had been home to Jeff Barrett's Phil Kaufman Club (named after Gram Parsons' famous road manager), but he had moved on and now Roger Cowell ran it, sitting at his little table where he took the money every night.

The in-house PA was owned by a long-haired fella called Pep, a geezer whose hippyish appearance belied a sharp, no-nonsense intelligence. Pep ran a company called Imps PA, and when he was busy with other jobs, like touring with George Melly & The Feetwarmers, he left the sound engineering at the Falcon to Andrew Hackett. Andy was a Norwich boy in his early to mid-20s, who hadn't been living in London all that long. An admirer of The Loft and The Weather Prophets, he recognised the unmistakable face of Dave Morgan as soon as we walked through the door together, and soon we were all mates. I told Andy I'd had a country rock band called The Rockingbirds and was going to start a new one. Hackett said he had always wanted to be in a country band and was well up for it. He was the guitarist in Milk and I knew he could play. I said, great, let's do it. It was as easy as that.

Andy knew everyone. His job gave him plenty of opportunities, of course, but he never let them go to waste. You could rely on Hackett to do most of the talking and make the running. I may have had some quiet arrogance and self-belief, I suppose, but that hardly endeared me to all, and I relied a lot on Hackett's self-confidence and blunt good humour to open doors for us. Hack rarely held back, and had a talent for social networking. He sometimes played on being a Norfolk country bumpkin. Like most of The Rockingbirds (myself the exception), he had left school at 16, but would make a point of letting you know he was a chap with some education: he had read a few books, and knew some big words, "like wheelbarrow and gooseberry".

Some could find Hackett's overtures annoying. When he'd first arrived in London, playing in a band and living in a squat, young Hack would turn up at the Phil Kaufman Club and try to get in with gifts of expensive cheese he had filched from Paxton & Whitfield, the Mayfair deli where he worked. Jeff may have grumbled at the time about "that bloke and his bloody cheese", but this was how our relationship with the guy who got us a major record deal began.

Hackett knew how to go through the gears and win people over. If you didn't find his jokes funny at first he would oblige you by repeating them until eventually you had to laugh. Resistance was futile; people would say "Who is this guy?" and the next time you saw them they'd be coming out of a two-day bender with him, bonded and buddied for life. I could never fail to be impressed. Hackett was an absolute Mountie.

Our headquarters, 123 Camden Road, was a crumbling Georgian-style double-fronted house with a porch with two columns and steps up to the big front door. Semi-detached, it stood next to 125, a house of identical design but in greater disrepair, and squatted. Our next-door neighbours were also in poorer physical condition. Our place was no drug-free zone, but in 125 they went at it harder than us, and if drugs could not be found or afforded, anything might be tried. One night, an ambulance arrived, and several of them were whisked off to hospital with nutmeg poisoning. Sometimes their occupant numbers became unmanageable and there was some camping in the grounds of the house to manage the overspill. One night, a couple who had improvised a bed on an upstairs landing next to an open window rolled out onto the paving below. They must have been in a "relaxed" state, as they survived without serious injury. At one point, one of the main guys living there, Dodgy Dave, proposed he knock a hole through the wall for a door to make our two houses into one. My answer was emphatically NO. Dave the Dodge had a noisy grunge band called Bum Gravy. Enough said. Bands like his didn't play at the Falcon; if they were lucky they might get a gig playing to their fellow 'crusties' at Club Dog at the George Robey in Finsbury Park.

Over the fence from the two houses was the respectable Camden School For Girls, where, at the end of the school day, local boys would gather like tomcats at the gates, waiting for the nice young ladies to emerge. One night, with all the girls gone to wherever they went, we lifted a panel in the fence and removed one of the school picnic tables to have in our kitchen. The next day, we waited to see the caretaker standing on the spot where the table had been, looking puzzled. (Thoughtfully, we put the table back when we moved out). The basement kitchen had been nothing more than an empty, stone-floored room with an electric cooker and a sink plumbed in; now, with the wooden picnic table, it became our main shared area for entertaining, day or night. Next door to the kitchen was the bathroom, another big, bare room with a bath and sink in the corner. This was where we rehearsed. Mercifully, there was a separate privy by the back door.

I had a main ground floor room, extending from the front of the house to the back, above the bathroom, and Dave had the other, above the kitchen. Upstairs, in similarly proportioned, airy, well-lit rooms, was a nice young woman called Sian and a good-looking gay motorcycle courier who rode a Moto Guzzi and knew Jarman. At the top in the attic, holding out for a Camden council flat, were Mary, from my old co-op, and the father of her baby-to-be, dope-dealing Den. That's how it stood when we first moved in, and a few people came and went over the next two years as our band activities progressively took over.

Our other residents, the mice, remained all the time we were there. In my room I affected to keep a green budgerigar called Popeye. Mice found their way into his cage and from time to time I would find the poor, perplexed bird with an unwanted visitor eating his seed. There was probably more food there for the hungry rodents than anywhere else in the house.

So Hackett was on board for my new country band, and Dave I had captured by giving him pride of place in our Camden castle. Dave was joined by his fiancée from Switzerland, Emmanuelle (the one who had usurped Phoebe), and they got spliced at Wood Green Civic Centre. It was a motley rock'n'roll wedding: Hackett in his tweeds, me in my cowboy clobber, Piece in his pinstripes looking relatively respectable, Dave in his leopard-skin jacket, and peroxide blonde Emmanuelle in her exquisitely-chosen 50s vintage gear. Her mother came over, bravely; her father, a Swiss banker, stayed away.

Emmanuelle Morgan was a lovely girl, delightfully charming and clever, but she was also, shall we say, young and a little wilful. She bought a dog, Elliot, without asking anyone in the house, and neither she nor Dave could train it. It barked and shat everywhere. She had a Vespa scooter (everything had to be stylish, stylish, stylish!) and rode it with scant regard for the rules of the road, up and down pavements, through red lights; her stint as a motorcycle courier did not last long. In short, she was a real crackerjack, and there were heated arguments, sometimes with me and others in the house, but mainly with Dave. During one of their noisy confrontations that continued long into the night, I lost it. I banged on their door and shouted at her to get out, and in the morning, Emmanuelle was gone. For good.

*

At first, we were not to be called The Rockingbirds; that was the name of the old band. The High Fences was considered, which we thought pretty good, but in the end it had to be The Rockingbirds. It was a name that could have been from 30 years ago, but somehow never was. A name that had some truth and poetry about it, I thought, but was not trying to be enigmatic or say too much. This was during the height of the fad for bands with ultra-wacky names; Half Man Half Biscuit, Ned's Atomic Dustbin, Carter the Unstoppable Sex Machine. I was against all that. In our world these acts were abominations, and their advocate Jon Fat Beast (RIP) was the antichrist. Rockingbirds suggested dinosaurs, stone age flying lizards. Pterodactyls appeared on our flyers and artwork. Ultimate retro.

But if we were to be The Rockingbirds, how did I tell the old ones? Dave Heley had broken his leg and had been out of action. Unfortunately we had rather fallen out in the final days at the old house, so I let that one lie. If Dave Morgan was in, then Phoebe, now very much his ex, was out. I presumed she would understand. We didn't have a bass player yet, but I didn't think Stan was right for the upgrade; we met for a drink, I told him something or other, and he was magnanimous and kinder to me than perhaps I deserved. Then there was Piece. This was the most difficult one, because he was very much still on the scene. Hackett had to be in, but we couldn't have three six-string guitarists in the band (me being the third); that was excessive.

Shamelessly, I telephoned Piece and told him I had to come and speak to him about a problem I had. Concerned, Piece said "Of course, come round pal". I then drank four cans of strong lager in quick succession to conquer my anxiety, got round to his place, and turned on the waterworks. Tearfully I explained to him that we were going to have to call it a day, and invited him to console me as I sobbed out the painful news, as if it was me that the gods had somehow wronged. Piece, bless him, kindly played along with my deceit. He patted me, gave me a bit of bog roll to dry my eyes, told me not to be so daft, and suggested we go down to the pub. Job done. He later made his true thoughts known by telling me he didn't think we were that good anyway, and the plaudits The Rockingbirds later received we "didnae deserve". Thanks, Piece. Fair comment. Possibly.

For a bass player, we turned to Sean Read. Sean was Hackett's best mate from Norfolk and was in London as the singer in his band, Milk. He wasn't a bass player, but Hack assured me he was a very clever lad who could play piano and various brass instruments, so likely he could learn bass, we thought, and contribute his singing talent into the mix.

The day I first met Sean can be given a precise date: it was Saturday 31 March, 1990, the day of the great poll tax riot in central London. Andy and I had intended to go along to the protest, being poll tax renegades ourselves, but Hack had come round to mine on the way that morning with a couple of microdots. We hatched them, and consequently spent the whole afternoon down a cosmic American rabbit hole with The Flying Burrito Brothers and the International Submarine Band. In the evening, Sean met us at the Falcon. Still spaced out, I first perceived his tall frame from behind as he stood at the bar. His jacket looked weird, its white and scarlet blotches morphing before my eyes, like a tie-dye. It turned out it was a plain white denim jacket, soaked in his own blood. He had been walloped on the head by a policeman's truncheon whilst rioting in Trafalgar Square.

We lent Sean a bass guitar and gave him a week to learn a handful of songs that we had on a tape. After the week was up we tried him out, but we had been over-optimistic about his power to master the new instrument. He had made a little progress on the first song, *Now You're On Your Own*, but none with the rest.

Disappointed, I thought it would still be nice to hear him singing harmonies with me. We tried *Love Has Gone & Made A Mess Of Me* and *Standing At The Doorstep Of Love* and it was a revelation. It blew me away, the blend of our voices was something else. His singing was so true and sure, so strong, and together we were more than the sum of our parts. Sean was in the band, both Hackett and I agreed without discussion; no question. He would be our Gene Clark, our Mister Tambourine Man.

The bass player vacancy was temporarily resolved by Paul Kingston, another East Anglian in London. We did one gig with Paul at the 101 Club in Clapham, which went OK, but he said he was making too much money in the building trade to be sidetracked. At that point we turned to Morgan's former Weather Prophets bandmate Dave "Greenwood" Goulding. I wonder now why we hadn't asked him sooner. I didn't know him all that well (I knew his brother Nigel better) but Dave Goulding was a charmer; urbane and handsome, a good bass player and a good bloke.

Five easy pieces, but one more was needed; to get that weapons-grade country rock sound for real, and really set us apart, we knew we had to get a steel player. Hackett, once again, knew one. Living in Norfolk, Patrick Arbuthnot was, we suspected, of fairly genteel stock, but he had left his posh school at the earliest opportunity to get a job making digger buckets. He had done some shifts in the past as a guitarist in Hank Wangford's band, but his interest in engineering found its natural object in the pedal steel guitar, one of the oddest musical contraptions known to man.

It seems crazy now that Patrick carried that heavy assemblage of wood and metal, AND his Peavey combo amp, on the train from Norwich, then on the tube and up the escalator at Camden Town station, and then on foot half a mile up Camden Road to our house, to get to our first rehearsal, but he did exactly that. Having arms like the limbs of an oak made it just possible. We nicknamed him "The Wise One" because of his wizard-like shock of silver hair.

We had done one gig at the Falcon before he joined, but were now looking forward to playing the Bull & Gate in Kentish Town with our exciting new addition. In the week of the gig Patrick had an accident on the lathe in his shed, slicing the top of one of his fingers off. Calamity! He was out of action. It was a blow, but undeterred we obtained the telephone number of BJ Cole, the UK's best-known pedal steel player, to see if he would step in. He agreed, and did the gig. BJ became a big friend and supporter from then on, and for our next gig The Wise One was on board and we were ready to fly.

So everything was going well. The Rockingbirds were country music missionaries, and we communicated our new-found music passion with a keen, punky urgency that won over the audiences. Over the next year or so we played the Falcon again, the White Horse 'Sausage Machine' in Hampstead and the Borderline, and we did our first out-of-town gig in Brighton, with others to follow further afield: Hull Adelphi, Leeds Duchess Of York, the Joiners in Southampton, venues on the so-called "toilet" gig circuit, reviled by many working musicians but loved by us. On one run out, I think it was after a gig at the Charlotte in Leicester, we decided to camp in some woods for want of proper accommodation. The campfire and the booze were fun, while they lasted, but living with our ash-dusted, unwashed selves the next day was a little grim.

For on the road entertainment, picking up hitchhikers was obligatory, if they could be squeezed in. Sometimes friendships would be struck and they would remain with us for the evening's gig or longer, but sometimes, if they proved too mental – like the one who opened the door while we were bombing down the M6 – they were given the slip at services.

At a certain point a truck-spotting game was invented, called "Atki". The rules of Atki were as follows: the first person to spot a Seddon Atkinson truck (British and best) got three points and became the caller. The caller nominated any make of truck, ERF, Volvo, Ford, Renault, whatever, and the first player to spot a nominated truck got one point. The caller remained the caller until someone else spotted an Atki, at which point they got three points and the call went to them. Foden trucks (the other esteemed British make) were the jokers, which won you two points at any time. It was a game played to the highest imaginable pitch of noisy competitiveness, which was great until the driver got involved too, fixing his attention on the distant badges of oncoming trucks in the rain rather than attending to the hazards in the road in front of him. When more spacious vans allowed us to play cards at tables and Atki was superseded by Bastard Brag for £1 antes, my motorway passenger anxieties were greatly relieved.

Being the only country rockers in Camden (or almost any other) Town, we were determined to signify our defiant difference by wearing clothes that set us apart from our grungy indie-rock contemporaries. On first setting foot in The Falcon I had collected a fair number of pearly-studded western shirts, easily found in Camden Market and the London vintage shops, and this was a look that Hackett quickly adopted. His suggestion that everyone in the band should do the same, however, was not uniformly obeyed, which I thought for the best. Unless done to the nth degree and with a high level of aplomb, "everyone wearing the same thing" is not a great look for a band, especially when you are matching embroidered cowboy shirts with the wrong kinds of jeans, imported from the Far East rather than the good old US of A. Sean and Dave Goulding (tall, fine looking fellows that they were) looked dandy in recently acquired secondhand satin numbers from Rokit, but I was happy that Morgan stuck with his lean, leopard print and leather look, which was more Cramps than cowpoke. Patrick, as I remember, had a special red buttonless creation for on-stage wear that had snakeskin detail and looked vaguely native-American, but he was too frugal to be coerced into buying any other clobber, new or not so new. He did have an eye-catching pair of turquoise pixie boots, but at his instrument he swapped these for the cheap Chinese slippers that were better for navigating his pedals.

Cowboy boots and hats were the other obvious go-tos for us country boys, but I was wary of cornball trappings. Hackett had a pair of western boots, which were ok; buff, rough and not too flamboyant, they avoided any fancy Kings Road excess that might put me in mind of David St Hubbins' embarrassing girlfriend in *Spinal Tap*. For footwear I stuck with Chelsea boots and a pair of elvish black suede slip-ons that I'd found at a jumble sale.

The correct footwear solution was to be found later when we got to Texas in 1992. Ropers are cowboy boots but less showy, with flat heels and no nasty chiselled tip at the toe, quite like Chelsea boots but more sturdy and with leather pull-ups instead of elastic side panels. Justin Ropers are the famous brand, and they sold them at Academy Sports & Outdoors, a big warehouse store a little drive out from Austin's city centre. This is where the band finally bought some big hats, and (along with the Ropers) it was where I located real Wranglers. Sung about by Jonathan Richman in his song "My Jeans" and preferred over the ubiquitous Levis, the desired US denims came rigid and unwashed with a plastic (not faux leather) tag. I bought a pair of regulars and a pair in the slightly flared boot cut style, each a snip at around $20. Wranglers and Ropers I made my thing, and I have worn them ever since.

But before and after we came by this authentic Americana, we liked to throw archetypally British pop fashion items like

Harrington jackets, Ben Shermans and Fred Perry shirts in with our western weaves. Ben Sherman were soon to start modernising and messing with their designs, but back then they still sold shirts that were identical to the ones worn by skinheads in the early 70s, with the same tartanesque prints, button-down collars, and the pleating and hanging loop up the back. Plaid lumber shirts and cords with an early 60s Dylan vibe also came into our Anglo-American, country-mod mashup. All in all, we were not being remarkably clever or creative, but it was, for the most part, pretty nice gear, and we liked it. Some of our choices perhaps entered more into the mainstream men's look as the years went by, but if they did, I shall not delude myself that we played much of a role as influencers on the tides of fashion.

*

At a Bull & Gate gig (and later the Borderline) we tried a new thing, the Rockingbirds Rolling Revue, where we invited musician friends to sing a country cover, with us as the backing band. Heidi Berry and her friend Sumishta sang *Fly Into The Mystery,* Lesley from Silverfish sang *Your Good Girl's Gonna Go Bad,* Tom from Th' Faith Healers sang Hank Williams' *Lovesick Blues,* Joss Cope (Julian's brother) did a number, and our eccentric rockabilly friend Chalky The Yorkie hiccupped through Ricky Nelson's *Lonesome Town*. Lesley and Tom's songs came out as a one-off single on Clawfist, our first record.

Also joining our show was a young acting student at RADA, Caroline Caplan, who had recently moved to London from

Manchester. Sitting by chance next to Andy Hackett on a bus going to a gig, our guitarist had been excited to identify the strains of Hank Williams leaking from the headphones of her cheapo Walkman. Before their ensuing conversation had ended, Andy had dreamed up a scheme to win an actor's union Equity card for his sparky new friend, by having her sing with our band at six paid gigs. The first of these (not paid, but whatever) was the Rolling Revue, duetting with me on the Gram and Emmylou song, *We'll Sweep Out The Ashes In The Morning*. In truth, the future *Doc Martin* telly star didn't need much of a leg up from us; she was soon in demand, and only had to change her name from Caplan to Catz to get her coveted work card. She did more gigs with us though (and with Monoland, her quirky folk combo), and by the time Dave Morgan moved in with her to share her little Carol Street co-op place, she was very much a full-on member of the Rockingbirds gang.

*

Jonathan Richman had a new album out, *Jonathan Goes Country*. Delighted to find my hero travelling in a similar musical direction to ours, I wrote a tribute song, *Jonathan Jonathan,* which told his story, mixed in with some of mine.

> *"When we saw your last show I was glad to see*
> *You can still be as good as you'll always be*
> *Now you play country music... a bit like me"*

I was working as a cycle courier for a company called Megacycles, based in Panther House, Mount Pleasant, EC1. Back then, before the internet, courier companies thrived in London, moving legal documents, photographs, architects' drawings, cheques and anything else urgent on cycles and motorbikes. I had been doing the job since my Bounds Green days, on a big steel-framed Raleigh that I had found in an abandoned co-op flat. My wheels were not the quickest, but building on my previous London knowledge, I got to know every street and how to get there, and delivered as swiftly as any boy racer.

Megacycles, run by two guys called Gerry, was a fun company to work for. There were cold Peronis in the office on Friday evenings, more drinks in The Thunderer afterwards, and the firm threw a huge party for its staff and clients at the Scala Cinema every Christmas. By now, I was not going to work as often as I used to. With no rent to pay I could get away with going in only two or three times a week, picking up about £25-£30 a day. You just called in on your radio in the morning when you wanted to work, but if you wanted to sleep in, nobody bothered you. I met Big Steve Pulford working at Megacycles, before he had success with The Arlenes. Big Steve was called Steve Tree in those days, or "Tree-Tree-Tree," as the controllers called him on the radio, to distinguish him from the other Steves on the road. He was getting a country/rockabilly band together, A-La-Tex, and was very much on our musical wavelength. He was also a driver, so we got him driving for The Rockingbirds.

One of Megacycles' clients, just a couple of blocks away on the corner of Hatton Garden and Clerkenwell Road, was Capersville, Jeff Barrett's press outfit. The business had grown out of his work with Creation Records, who occupied the same office building. Our band had Jeff and his fledgling label Heavenly very much in our sights; his Phil Kaufman Club moniker was an early indication he might take an interest in our maverick country enterprise. Some of his closest associates, including Spencer Smith and Martin Kelly from the band East Village, were already coming to Rockingbirds gigs, sometimes with Jeff's girlfriend, Val, an early fan. Spencer, the drummer, was in the Falcon a lot, the Hawley even more, and if not there he was nearer his home in Portobello, at the Lonsdale, necking the Sam Smith's Alpine Lager. Spence loved Dylan, and had all the records. He was also a great admirer of our Dave, and admitted later that he fell out of love with the Rockingbirds a little bit when Morgan left. We forgave the boy for his honesty.

Martin was working with Jeff on the new label. They were fans of Gram and fans of 80s country stars Dwight Yoakam and Nanci Griffith. We had to get Jeff to come and see us. Martin agreed. In the end Jeff didn't come to a gig, he came to the house to hear us play in the bathroom.

The whole band assembled at the appointed time, but Jeff and Martin were late. Jeff, Martin later confided, was having a cash flow crisis; he was broke, and hadn't wanted to come out that night to hear any good news from The Rockingbirds that might commit him to spending more of his non-existent money. In the end, Martin prevailed, and Jeff showed up. We played a couple of songs, *Doorstep* (Jeff nodded his assent, "Good") *Jonathan Jonathan* (more assent from Jeff, "Good, really good song!") and then we played a couple more, and then they were off again. Martin said he'd let us know. He let us know the next day: Jeff wanted us to do a single on Heavenly. Yess!

Pete Astor was an easy choice of producer. He was someone most of us knew and liked, and he knew his way around a studio. He recommended Bark in Walthamstow, where he had been recording his new album, a stone's throw away from his house. Bark was run by Brian O'Shaughnessy, who had recorded The Firm's novelty No 1 *Star Trekkin'*. With DJ producer Andrew Wetherall he had also had a hand in the making of Primal Scream's *Loaded*, the seminal single that heralded the coming of *Screamadelica* in 1991.

The indie dance movement that Primal Scream became leaders of was a seismic thing at that time, both for the music scene widely and for the band, whose fortunes completely changed. A few months before the release of *Loaded*, I had been intrigued to see that the Primals were booked to play at the Plough in Kenton, the pub local to my old home and north London secondary school. A gig in Kenton? Strange, I thought. Dave Morgan, Dave Goulding and Hackett came with me to see it, with prehistoric Rockingbird

Stan and our mate Kevin also coming along. Dave and Dave knew Primal Scream from the Creation days; Morgan had been their drummer, for a while, in '87. The large, landmark pub next to the Kenton Grange where many of my teachers had consumed lunchtime pints was now fully revamped as a rock venue. Some foolhardy dreamer had invested heavily in a well-equipped stage and PA system and had covered the walls with rock memorabilia, posters and photographs where once had been faux horse brasses and hunting scenes.

The Primals came on to do their hard-rocking long-hair schtick with songs from their second album. They put on a good show, under the circumstances, but there was no one there; just us, the band, and the staff. Not being near any tube or railway station it was an unlikely place for a venue, but no one? It was harsh. As the gods of rock gazed down at them in mute judgement from the photos on the walls, I felt sorry for Primal Scream, I really did. I was convinced that it was all over for them. I was wrong. In a few months their fortunes were transformed, as their glorious butterfly burst forth from its grebo cocoon.

Primal Scream taught me one important lesson – which, I have to admit, I have never had the professionalism to fully live by. I was friendly with Tim Tooher, who worked in Rock On Records in Camden along with our artist mate Ski Williams, the singer from Hippies With Muscles. Like Ski, Tim was an uber-music fan with an encyclopaedic knowledge a level above the rest of us. Tim later had a big hand in steering the Primals' post-*Loaded Dixie Narco* adventures with Jim Dickinson. Back then he was sharing a flat in Camden with Bobby Gillespie and others in the band, and they had just had an *NME* front cover. I went round there with Tim to pick up a book or a record or something. The place was an absolute tip. Unwashed crockery and cutlery and takeaway boxes and bits of food lay piled up everywhere, as if nothing had ever been cleaned or tidied away from the day they had moved in. I glanced around and realised they lived according to a law that up until then I had not properly understood: *rock stars NEVER do the washing up.*

Another lesson I still had to learn was how to take the new drugs. Jeff invited us out to a pub in Wendover, where his friends were putting on an all-day rave with Andrew Weatherall and the Primals in attendance. It was a hot summer's day, and a lot of us Rockingbirds were there. Caroline came with Dave, I think, and I brought someone too. Fair-haired Go-Betweens fan Anna Hobley was a regular at the Falcon, where she had taken a shine to The Rockingbirds, and, as my good luck would have it, to me. We arrived together at the Wendover venue, got a bottle of beer each, and then she and I took our first Es. Half an hour later, the two of us were underneath a table, literally, huddled together, completely freaked out by the potency and alien rush of the drug and in a state of absolute resistance to it. Despite all the ecstatic fun that was going on around us, we were desperate to escape, and finally found our sorry way back to the railway station, longing for the effects to wear off.

It was quite a long time before I tried ecstasy again, and I always made sure I had a few beers inside me when I did, to cushion the impact. I could enjoy parties and dance events like the Heavenly Sunday Social in later years, but I was never going to be a raver.

*

At Bark we recorded *A Good Day For You Is A Good Day For Me, Jonathan Jonathan,* plus *Restless* and a cover of Alex Chilton's *Free Again*, which was in our live set. The first two were good, but I didn't think the other two – one of which we needed to choose for the third track – were standing up. I had a few days before mixing, and thought I'd try to pick something out of the air, and write something fresh and simple that could be recorded quickly without setting up the drums again. I asked myself "what shall I write about?" and my answer was, "write about the most important thing in the world". So I wrote *Only One Flower*.

> *"There's only one flower that grows in my garden*
> *There's only one sun that shines in my sky*
> *And there's only one star that shows in my darkness*
> *Only one road I travel by"*

I ran through it with just Dave Goulding on bass and Sean doing backing vocals, and we opened Bark Studios for a couple of hours on the Saturday morning to record it as a live take. Pete opened the door so the mics picked up the street noise outside, birds tweeted and a car went by, and Brian cranked the EQ to make it sound vivid and trebly, like *Rock'n'roll With The Modern Lovers*. Dave, Sean and I caught the song perfectly on the first or second take, and I was delighted with the result. Others liked it too, but I knew it was walking a line between cool and fool. Hackett, I sensed, didn't think much of my little *fait accompli*, which was more of a 'personal statement' than a band effort, more a prayer-like poem than a song. After we played it live, a song that he and Dave Morgan sat out, Hackett observed (in case I hadn't noticed) that some in the audience had been sniggering.

Jeff wanted *Jonathan Jonathan* to be the A-side, but I disagreed. Jeff should have insisted. Officially it was a double-A single, but with *Jonathan Jonathan* sharing a side of vinyl with *Only One Flower, A Good Day For You* appeared as the *de facto* A-side. It was a mistake, because *Jonathan* was a way better song, but I couldn't see this at the time. I thought it being a tribute song narrowed its appeal. I ignored the fact that The Family Cat had had a long-running indie No 1 with *Tom Verlaine*, another homage to a US punk hero. Anyway, I didn't care about the indie charts, which was just as well, because our first single proper did not trouble them. Cathi Unsworth shot *Good Day* down with an imaginary Uzi in her *NME* singles review.

Ever since I'd started reading the music papers I had daydreamed of being interviewed about my own group, but when the opportunity finally came I found it more difficult than I thought it was going to be. My well rehearsed inner monologues would invariably dissolve into the ether when a journalist asked me his first question, and I would find myself, Rupert Pupkin-like, with nothing much to say. Luckily the rest of the band would save the day with all the matey bonhomie and tall tale telling a scribe could wish for, but I came to slightly resent these amusing distractions from my ineffable mission.

In later days, after The Rockingbirds reformed, I once suggested to Sean that I adopt a policy of enigmatic absence, staying out of interviews altogether. He sympathised and thought it was not a bad idea, which was the wrong response. I did not welcome confirmation that I could be awkward and remote in front of journalists, even if I had asked for it.

*

With the single coming out, we were taken on by our first gig agency. Perhaps not by coincidence, they were also Jonathan Richman's agents, and they were booking a short UK tour for him; would we be able to support him, we asked? I thought it was unlikely; on recent visits, Jonathan's shows had been opened by jugglers and comics, which makes reasonable sense when you are a quiet, solo performer. You don't want to be blasted off by a noisy band playing before you.

Jonathan, to my delight, agreed to have us along. It was our first national tour, and we were supporting my all-time favourite artist, who we had just written and recorded a tribute to. It was all so wonderfully right; our appointment with destiny. But I wasn't sure about how to let him hear the song, and I left it out of the set, in case he heard some of it and didn't like it, or misunderstood. It seemed presumptuous to put it out there without finding out how he felt about it, but it also wasn't fair to ask him permission or something like that, to put him on the spot. It was his gig and his tour. I left it.

Backstage he kept himself to himself, which was fair enough. He had an exercise workout he used to do. At one venue there was a big backstage area, and he was doing his exercises at one end of the room, and there was just me at the other end, tuning up my guitar. I started quietly playing *Only One Flower* while he did his push-ups and squats. I was hoping a vain hope that he would pick up on my gentle song and poetical lyrics and show some interest, but he just ignored me.

The tour went well. We were on our best behaviour. The last date was at London's Mean Fiddler, which was always to prove a great gig for us, that night and on subsequent visits. Our shows all done, Jonathan sat down for a while with us backstage, and we relaxed and chatted for the first time. I seized my chance, and told him we had something that we'd like him to hear. I put the cassette in the boogie box, and our song began...

> *"Jonathan I remember you said*
> *When you first heard Heroin*
> *That you'd never heard a thing so beautiful*
> *That it nearly did you in..."*

"That's right, I did say that," confirmed Jonathan, lighting up and taking notice. And as his story went on in my song, as he followed the Velvets wherever they'd go, and as he bummed around and played his surf guitar all day in California, and as he hung out with Gram and shook my hand at the Hammersmith Odeon, Jonathan affirmed these moments from his life, as sung about by me, with nods, laughs and "Yups". I had my prize, and my happiness was complete. *Jonathan Jonathan* was not to be a chart hit, but my song was bang on target.

*

1991 was drawing to a close. Christmas was coming. Andy Hackett was always on the lookout for "a little earner". Our mate from the Falcon, known to all as Strobe, was now living at 123. His parents had a small forest of conifers on land next to their house in Devon, grown to be sold as Christmas trees, that they had thus far failed to harvest. I knew this, I had been down there, and had observed that the forest was too densely planted and now hopelessly overgrown, with scrawny-looking trees greatly inferior to the fat-needled specimens you saw on sale in town.

My warnings were not heeded, and Hackett and Strobe made the trip down to Devon with Big Steve, returning with a Transit van full of trees. As fate would have it, a TV news item on the day of their return reported a glut of Christmas trees in London that year. Oh dear! Perhaps a little smugly, I sat back to watch them try to interest the local retailers in taking their not-so-green evergreens, already shedding needles wherever they went. With the predicted lack of success, the trees went into the front garden, and a sign was put up to advertise they were for sale, cheap. We took no callers;

maybe people were frightened off by the Munsters-like menace of our house, or maybe it was just the trees. Hackett and Strobe donated the best one they had to a local school, and got a nice thank you letter from the headmistress.

After Christmas, we threw a New Year's Eve party. We didn't bother to spruce the place up, but with Christmas trees the main decoration, the party had an invigorating, pine-fresh atmosphere. Lots of old friends came, from Norfolk to Noel Park, along with people from the Falcon, Camden and round about. Some Primal Screams looked in. Regular house visitors Pete Astor and Lawrence from Felt (now recording his first Denim album at Bark with Sean) were likely there, along with a journalist or two – we even let a few of them in from next door. The party was gossiped about the following week in *True Stories* in the *NME,* which made implausible claims about a few other well-known attendees, including Blur, who had shown up at four in the afternoon (so it said), drunk and far too early, and then disappeared. The new year was going to be OUR BIG YEAR.

Agoristo

EARLY IN 1992 I had a dream, and it told me three things: Agoristo, number 14, and Devon & Exeter – a name, a number, and a racecourse. I had dreamt a winning horse.

In junior school our regular teacher was sick one afternoon and a new one took our class. It was the Grand National that weekend, and Mr Webber improvised a lesson on horse racing and gambling, explaining how odds were calculated and how to read the form in the back of the newspaper. It was the single most interesting and educational hour I ever spent at school. Since then, I have liked a gamble, now and then, whenever something pricks my interest. It doesn't happen often; I have a bet only once every couple of years, on average. Honest.

I may be a self-declared singer-songwriting failure, but I am not an all-round loser. Habitual betting is a fool's pastime. You don't need evidence to appreciate this, but I have seen plenty of such evidence in my time. In my student days I worked in Hector McDonalds, a big chain of north London betting shops, usually as a cashier but sometimes, when the monitors conked out, as a boardman, writing up the odds on the boards as they came over the Tannoy. The firm would pay out on the odd well-judged wager, but the great majority of their customers bet blindly on numbers and hunches, on rumours passing for "tips", and so were easily relieved of their money on a daily basis. The staff knew little better. In those days it was easy to place bets while at work, and we did; a blind eye was turned by most managers as long as our tills balanced at the end of the day. The managers were even less scrutinised, and could take greater liberties. On two different occasions I came in to work to find the manager had not shown up: unable to make up the mounting deficit of Hector McDonald's takings that they had gambled away, these managers would do a runner.

I do gambling in much the same way I have done strong drugs; I get in for a quick win if things are being given away or if the conditions seem favourable, and then retire to a safe distance for an extended period of abstinence. Leaving aside card games among friends (Bastard Brag on the tour bus, £10 ante limit poker nights) where money usually passes pleasantly back and forth without great profit or loss to anyone, winning has the same effect on me as losing; both outcomes make me unwilling to bet again, and I walk away. Bookmakers and casinos set the odds to give themselves an edge over their punters, which means in the long run the law of averages will always assert itself, so it is only for a quick hit and run that gambling can be justified. My guiding principle has always been to go in fairly strongly when something appears much more likely to occur than the bookmakers realise; which is to say, when they have miscalculated the odds and you have the edge.

I've only ever visited one racecourse, the Aqueduct, on my 80s New York trip. The brown dirt track on that grey day made for a colourless spectacle, and I made but one miserly and uninspired bet. I have long fancied going to an English race meeting in a verdant country setting; it would make a lively, colourful day out, I am sure, but so far I never have. Train fares and course entrance fees put me off racecourse betting, as these represent unnecessary initial losses that need to be recouped by winnings if the gambling is to be genuinely successful.

Bookmakers now urge their customers to "gamble responsibly" and to stop betting when the "fun" ends. This hypocrisy, shifting the ethical burden from the business to the customer, misrepresents gambling, the primary purpose of which is not fun; but winning. I have had two large payouts in my lifetime, along with smaller wins. My memory may have glossed over a few lost wagers but on the strength of those two big wins alone I know I have won more than I've lost. I may yet be lured into some recklessness in the future to annul all my past profits. Some will say that all gamblers are bound to lose in the end, but this assumes that chance is directed by some higher and inevitable justice, which is not true: sometimes the punter really does come out the winner.

Would my dream horse present itself in reality? I went to the nearby betting shop that morning to find out. I had great expectations, but there was no Devon & Exeter meeting. I looked the next day, and again there was nothing that corresponded to my dream. After that, I forgot about it. After all, it was only a dream.

But one afternoon, as I passed Ladbrokes on Camden Road, I remembered to have another look. This time there *was* a Devon & Exeter meeting, with only one race with more than 14 runners, which had already run. Up on the screen I read that in the 2.35, the number 14 horse, Rags To Riches, had come in the winner. Though not a perfect anagram, all of the letters in Agoristo can be found in Rags To Riches. Wow, I thought. As a matter of fact, in my excitement I had misread the name, which was Road To Riches, not Rags. It lacked the "G" of Agoristo, but still not far off – and Devon & Exeter and the number 14 could not be mistaken. It was annoying to have walked into the betting shop too late to make a profitable bet, but I still marvelled that my dream horse had come true.

From then on, Agoristo became a thing for me, a magic, dream thing. It sounded like a place, a place I was going to, maybe in Texas, home to so many of my musical inspirations. Agoristo was a Shangri La, a final destination, a lost world, a promised land, a prophecy. From rags to riches... on the road to riches...

The name testified to our improving fortunes. Jeff was negotiating a label deal for Heavenly with Rob Stringer, head of A&R at Columbia, part of the Sony conglomerate. The Rockingbirds were going to be part of that deal, which meant a fully-funded recording budget to pay for the best studios and the producer of our choice, plus substantial cash advances for each of us. There was also a publishing deal in the offing, which was to be more lucrative for me, the songwriter. Jeff ended up getting £60,000 out of Warners; he took a cut as his reward, I took half of what was left, and the band shared the other half. Not a massive deal – Take That got a £250,000 publishing advance that year – but it was big to me.

After years of the dole, busking, student grants and shitty jobs, I would have more cash than I had ever seen. I was on the road to riches indeed. Jeff was doing a great job in getting everyone interested in the group; we had an album to make and TV and radio to do, and bigger gigs and the main festivals coming our way. Dreams were coming true, and I decided the album had to be called *Agoristo*. For a while, it was going to be.

Once the deal was in the bag we could start on the album, which was to be produced by Clive Langer at Westside, the studio in west London he co-owned with Alan Winstanley. The pair had made their fortunes recording hits for Madness and Dexys Midnight Runners. The Dexys connection was a big selling point for us; Sean and Andy were great fans, as was I. With only one single proper, we were still fairly naive about recording, or at least I was. Now we would work with respected pros who were in the habit of making hit records.

I made a big thing about wanting the recording to be "as live as possible". The affable and companionable Clanger went along with this, knowing that once we were in the studio we could be persuaded to go his way. He joined us for a week of pre-production at the Easyhire rehearsal place in Islington, and our keyboard-playing buddy, Zeben Jameson, who had been touring with The Pretenders, was brought in for the recording sessions. Our songs were already fairly tightly arranged, which left Clive less scope for his own innovations, but he came up with useful ideas for *Gradually Learning,* and a transformative key change for *Time Drives The Truck.*

By now 123 Camden Road had been taken back by its housing association owners. Sean had been living there at the end, and he and Strobe and some others broke into and squatted a shop-fronted house in the Angel, Islington: 321 St John Street, as numerological chance would have it. I got rehoused for a while in Dalston. St John Street, with its well-appointed bar in the front room, became our new HQ. From here the band travelled each day to Latimer Road tube to get to Westside. The studio was only a short distance from where I had first recorded at Street Level; things were much changed now.

I had a grandiose idea to re-record *Only One Flower* with the Chalk Farm Salvation Army Band, the band my grandad had been in. Being the backing vocalist and tambourine player, Sean didn't have a lot to do in the early stages of recording, so he occupied himself at a piano in a side room composing and scoring a full brass band arrangement. We couldn't get the Chalk Farm Band (who reserved their services for A Higher Power) but a good amateur band was hired, and on an evening towards the end of the sessions the players assembled in the live room and were given their various parts as written out by Sean. With only one or two minor corrections, the arrangement went to tape in no time. It was heavenly perfection, and I was deeply impressed. He was a clever lad, our Sean, as had been previously observed.

Our recording extravagances were not over. In June, after we'd finished recording the band, Jeff Barrett, Clive Langer and myself flew out to Austin, Texas to record horns, banjos and other instruments with The Bad Livers and other musicians at Arlyn Studios. At the helm would be "Texas" Mike Stewart. Clive had worked with Mike before on one of his less well-known production projects, an album by an Austin band called Poi Dog Pondering.

We arrived at 11pm Texas time (4am in London) and, too excited to turn in, I left Jeff and Clive at the hotel and wandered off into the hot Austin night, checking out every band in every bar I could find open on Sixth Street. That trip was the best time, the most amazing time for me. I loved working with those musicians, playing my songs in Willie Nelson's studio. All these things I had wanted, coming into being.

Part of me is always a bit lost, though, and I kept thinking about Agoristo. I had been thinking, "When this recording is done, then that's it... what then? Where to?" My vision did not extend further than the making of the record. It was the limit and entirety of my ambition, my all in all. Like the singular flower, bird, ocean and land in my song, there was to be *only one album*. With everything of mine now recorded, my work was done.

I succumbed to a romantic, fatalistic and vain idea; Agoristo was my destiny. I needed to find out where it was, while I was in Texas, and go there. It might be a town... or might it be a restaurant? Or a bar? I looked in the telephone directory and an atlas, but there was nothing. I asked Texas Mike, expecting him to say "Oh, yeah!" but he had never heard of it. Maybe I just had to walk out and disappear into the desert to find it, like Harry Dean Stanton in *Paris, Texas*. I looked for the desert, but there is no desert to walk out into from Austin, just fences with arable land beyond. There was no 'nowhere' to go to or disappear into. Agoristo was not to be found, so on the last day I got on the plane to go home with the others, as I was always going to do.

A few weeks later we returned to Austin to shoot the *Gradually Learning* video, this time with the whole band, and I was able to share with them my new-found love of Austin, staying in the same nice hotel on Congress with a pool, going to great gigs every night at places like The Broken Spoke, Henry's and the Continental, and buying old records, American clothes and other cowboy treasure. Terry Staunton from the *NME* came and joined us; together, we broke a margarita-drinking record at some restaurant, which got written about in *The Austin Chronicle* – and the *NME*, of course. We had a high time making that video, with Jeff Barrett walking on stilts, Goulding in cricketing gear, and Hackett on a horse. But still I succumbed to melancholy moments, and was missing Anna, who I'd split up with before we signed our deal. When I got back to London, we got back together, rented a place, and I asked her to marry me, and she said yes.

*

So much was happening in a short space of time. We had Glastonbury at the end of June, preceded by a short tour with The House of Love. Jeff said we needed to get a proper tour manager, so Terry McQuade, the former Clash roadie who had done some kind of road managing for our labelmates Flowered Up, was sent out with us. Terry had these huge sheets of paper which had everything on the tour planned and mapped out on a grid; old-fashioned spreadsheets, I guess they were, which served (if nothing else) to signal just how well organised and on the case he was.

The demand for greater professionalism was matched by an equal or even greater impulse on our part to go rogue. I was not a great fan of The House of Love (or any of their indie rock ilk) and it seemed from the first gig that the headline act's fans were not going to fall easily for our country enchantments. After a debate about how we might make a better connection, I decided to take an E and do a "talking gig", so the following night our set was a lot of ecstasy-induced loved-up bonhomie from me, punctuated by only four completed songs. In my happy mood I thought I had done a fair job of communicating the true meaning of love to the House Of Love's audience, and a couple pointing and laughing at me afterwards showed I had made some kind of an impression.

Most times it wasn't me who took the lead in band shenanigans. I was more the eye in the Rockingbirds storm, with other band members grabbing the initiative to create havoc around me. As we set off for Glastonbury, following some hard partying to celebrate the last House Of Love date the night before, I was feeling less than lively. Terry, on the other hand, seemed quite excited, excited to be *our* manager and glad not to be running around with Flowered Up anymore, who it turned out he had had a falling out with. Flowered Up were going to be at Glastonbury too, a fact which seemed to increasingly preoccupy him, but he'd be alright, he said, he was with a serious outfit now. The Rockingbirds were bigger lads than they were... and so he went on, as if we were going to fight his battles for him.

It was a hot, high summer day, and on the way to the festival we stopped off in a West Country town and followed our chaps-wearing lead guitarist into a large and well-stocked toy shop. Flushed with our recently acquired advances from Sony, nearly everyone in the band splashed out on the most extravagant Super Soaker water guns that the shop had to offer. The only ones who went without shooters were myself and Patrick; the Wise One was not one to splash out on anything.

Thus armed with all guns loaded, the pistol-packing Rockingbirds alighted in the backstage area of the Glastonbury Acoustic Stage firing at will, spraying everyone in range with jets of water. Meanwhile, I quietly slipped backstage to check our drinks rider. Unsurprisingly, these comedy cowboy scenes were not well appreciated by the folkies who ran the stage. One of them, a woman in a black leather bikini top, returned fire with a volley of rural obscenities. "It all went wrong for them when Dylan went electric," quipped the onlooking Jeff Barrett. It was a far-fetched explanation for her rage at us giving her tits a soaking.

After our mid-afternoon stage slot we dispersed into the festival, taking whatever alcohol we could carry but leaving the minibus backstage. The next day, concerns were being raised: tour manager Terry had disappeared... and where was our money? I ventured back towards the van with little Rob Brookes, our friend from the Falcon who now DJed and crewed for us, but before getting to the vehicle we were briskly accosted by Acoustic Stage staff and frogmarched into the production tent. There the stage manager did a fair job of intimidating us. Stabbing his finger at our chests, he told us that our band was "a fucking disgrace", that he would see to it that we would never play in the West Country ever again, and if we didn't get our van off his site in 45 minutes, they would break into it and move it themselves.

Dismissed from this kangaroo court, and gazing round the enormity of the festival, Rob and I realised that finding our driver to move the van in the space of just 45 minutes was a fool's errand, so we left them to do their worst. The good news was the money was in an envelope inside, but Terry, who had perhaps thought he'd lost it, was gone for good. It was presumed he had found his way back to his Flowered Up fold and made peace with his own people. Our driver Dave Evans, who I had known in his Twelve Cubic Feet days before his stint in the Mary Chain, took over Rockingbirds tour management for a while.

*

People had gently talked me out of calling the album *Agoristo*. I settled on *The Rockingbirds,* and vowed to myself that future albums by the band must have that eponymous element. Ski did the cover, a painstakingly-painted photograph of us on the doorstep of 123 Camden Road, embellished with pterodactyl bones and English roses. This was great, but Sony's corporate graphics people set about messing up what else they could. The title on the spine of the CD was so small you could barely read it, and the six paragraphs of a prose poem I had written for the inner sleeve were placed in a different order, on the whim of the designer. It was a trifle, of course, only I cared, but I was *so* pissed off, and rightly.

The Rockingbirds was greeted with fabulous reviews in the UK music press. A great fuss was made of my songwriting in particular, and I was thoroughly flattered. The *NME* gave the album a 9/10 review. Terry Staunton said he'd wanted to give it 10/10, but his editor had demanded he write another 500 words to justify that, so he had acquiesced. Columbia couldn't believe their luck; they had never had album debutantes with such a press reception. The PR department did a promo poster with the word "LEGENDARY" along the top, which had quotes from all the great reviews. At the end of the year, the *NME* writers voted *The Rockingbirds* one of their top 20 albums. It wasn't bad for a first go.

The good press, however, didn't translate into commercial success. Album sales were moderate, and *Gradually Learning* didn't chart, and neither did the follow-up single, a re-recorded

Jonathan Jonathan. Radio was patchy; Annie Nightingale liked us, but she only had a dance music show on Radio 1, and we were not that. We occupied a strange limbo-realm between pop and indie. Peel didn't like us, and didn't play us. I had expected he wasn't going to like us, and I had been right. I still maintained a disregard for rock, and indie especially, so I expected no sympathy from that genre's greatest champion.

Not all the press was positive; some suggested we were over-hyped, a "press band", and Cathi Unsworth attacked us again for embracing sentimentality and missing the "dark, melancholy irony" that made country music good. There was something in both criticisms. Jeff had done a fabulous job of hyping us... perhaps too good. But what could we do? It was hardly our fault. And yes, I was not focused on the darkness on the underside of existence that some found so vital and fascinating. That was for the goths, we thought, which was its own minefield of cliché and silliness. The dark stuff? All in good time.

*

We had concerns about Dave Goulding. He seemed to be going off the rails, not on the ball and making more than his fair share of mistakes on stage. We convened a little meeting about it, without Goulding, but with Jeff. Nothing was decided: we'd keep an eye on things. Was there any justice in this? Or was it scapegoating? Both, I'd say, but more of the latter. If Dave made more mistakes than anyone else, it was only a symptom of a bigger problem that we had no intention of facing up to.

Though we had signed with Sony for the world, only the UK territory had released the album. Absolutely nothing had happened in Europe, release-wise, and apart from a shitty review in a French mag ("la petite maison dans la prairie") we were ignored abroad. A release in Japan was mooted, but I never saw conclusive evidence. No releases in other countries meant no gigs there.

We did get asked to play in Sweden, however. At short notice we were asked to stand in for Billy Bragg at the Hultsfred Festival, with a nice slot quite high up the bill on the first day.

The trip started badly. We had been told to be at St John Street at a certain time without fail, to make our charter flights from Stansted to Sweden, but an hour after the appointed time we were still waiting for everyone to show. It wasn't unusual for tour managers to tell bands to be there before they needed to be, but I thought this morning we were bound by the charter flight time. Finally everyone arrived, but I was exasperated and assumed we were missing the flight. I had a bad feeling about it all. I had never liked that Billy Bragg bloke; he was another offender against my mother's "sing nicely or not at all" edict, which I righteously (if selectively) upheld. This one did not have our names on it.

We hadn't missed the plane, though it would have been better if we had. I knew that alcohol was expensive in Sweden, so I bought a couple of bottles of whiskey duty-free, and cracked one open on the flight. Andy Hackett did the same. Thus loaded, we landed on an airstrip in a forest. Everyone on the plane, all bands and their crews and hangers-on, got off and waited out on the tarmac in the sun. A crowd of fans had gathered on the other side of the perimeter fence to look at us pop stars. No longer knowledgeable about the artists of the day, I only recognised Damon Albarn out of Blur. Other bands playing the festival, like Primal Scream, had booked their own flights.

We waited and waited for a long time in the sun, with Andy and me taking swigs from the bottle. It was taking so long because the Swedish authorities were making a thorough search of everyone, regardless of who they were. We were one of the last to be checked; they went through everything. One of us had a wrap of something, and feared the worst when he was made to empty the contents of his wallet onto the customs officers' table. Stupidly, they didn't recognise the very thing they had been so thoroughly searching for, and so eventually everything and everyone was waved through. Already absolutely shitfaced, we got on a coach, which drove off into the forest. Then the coach broke down, and I remember Zeben and I getting out and making drunken attempts to push it.

A replacement coach finally got us to the festival. I was personally greeted and attended to by a charming and very attractive young American woman who worked for Warners, the generous publishers who had just signed us. I did my best to pull myself together and make a decent impression on her, in that ridiculous way, no doubt, that hammered people do when they try in vain to look sober. I had sufficient control of my mind to notice we had got our full rider – not only all the food, beer, wine and spirits we always asked for, but also the cigarettes, the truckers magazines and our rider's joke item, the guarana tablets. Such generous hospitality: a first. We were unable to return this kindness with any appropriate gratitude.

Once the ironically intended "hello Sweden"s were out of the way, our performance was a shambolic, drunken mess. Though Billy Bragg has since given me no cause to regret disparaging comments we may have made about him from the stage, we failed to offer our audience any refreshing alternative to the Bard from Barking, and a healthy crowd soon wandered off in puzzlement or disgust. Dave Goulding did some wandering himself, putting his bass down during a song to chat with the monitor man, and I did little better, straying from and then abandoning my own lyrics and chords. Only Hackett made no mistakes, or so he told me, and I believed him, for what it was worth.

After the show, we found our way back to the hotel, with the exception of Goulding, who had gone missing. He reappeared the next day. A cab had taken him to another town, miles away, and he had made his bed in the middle of a railway track somewhere, to be roused and rescued in the morning by a concerned passerby. The return flight wasn't till Sunday, so we had to see out the intervening time at the hotel and the festival. Disappointingly, my Warners lady had made herself scarce, Dave Morgan was clocking up an astonishing £690 in phone calls to Caroline from his room, and at some point that weekend I told Dave Goulding he was sacked.

On Sunday all the bands reassembled near the airport. Again there was much waiting around on tarmac, this time a car park. Hackett had acquired a skateboard, or maybe some kind of equipment trolley he was using as a skateboard, and was tormenting Dave Gedge of The Wedding Present with it, and teasing him for not having hits. I cringe to think of it now: The Wedding Present made it into the charts many times after that, and we never did. We were getting on everyone's wick, and more than just a little.

Everyone was to be fed in a large dining hall, and we seemed to be the last to be invited in. The Rockingbirds made their entrance together, a diabolical seven, and strolled down the aisle between the tables where everyone else had begun eating. The gentle hubbub of conversation subsided for a moment, then came a brief silence, then something happened: something got thrown. Was it one of us? Probably. Whatever it was, the next second the hall erupted into a massive food fight. It was absolute mayhem.

In this fight I did not participate. I stepped through the uproar and flying food in a kind of dream and went outside into the quiet of the afternoon, with the sun beating down, no-one around, and just the muted racket coming from inside, behind the door I had just shut behind me. In the car park in front of me was a coach, which I took to be ours. Once inside it, I realised it wasn't our coach at all, but in a seat like mine I found a bottle of Johnny Walker whisky just like mine, and I stole it.

Recollections after that are patchy, it was all in and out of consciousness, you understand. On the plane, some of us were subdued, but Sean Read was getting leery; he grappled with a plane door and had to be restrained by cabin staff. An argument then kicked off between Sean and the girlfriend of one of The Godfathers, and then with the entire band. This carried on after landing. At Stansted I shared a monorail car with Dave Goulding on the way to customs. It was just me and him in the carriage; he was naked, absolutely stark bollock naked, apart from his cowboy boots. He was in a friendly enough mood with me though, despite his being sacked; nothing untoward, nothing unusual. As my nude companion and I entered the "Nothing to Declare" area together, I saw spots of fresh blood on the floor. It was Sean's; one of The Godfathers had lamped him.

The dust-up was reported in one of the music papers, with an apology of some kind offered by Jeff on behalf of us and the label. Tales of this kind we recounted with an uneasy mix of remorse and glory. Getting mentioned in the papers was always a prime directive, but this story did us dubious credit.

*

With Goulding gone, Sarah Corina from The Mekons stood in to play bass for the next few gigs. Chris Clarke, who had worked reliably on Pete Astor's solo stuff, was auditioned and became Dave G's permanent replacement, which steadied the ship. The main drawback with Chris was his ginger hair; there were now two of us in the band. Could a band survive such a style disadvantage? If an error it was, it was one Chris and I would persist with long after the demise of The Rockingbirds.

Fiddle player Joolie Woods was also, unofficially, in the band. She had played on our self-produced B-side *Where I Belong* (one of our best efforts, I thought) and had turned up at Glastonbury. Now she was showing up at most gigs, and was kind of an item with Hackett, so I let it slide. Joolie was a good sport and a capable player, but I didn't really want her in the band, partly because she was another mouth to feed on the road, but mainly because her playing could clash with Patrick's. Pedal steel guitar veers in and out of tune at the best of times, but with fiddle, another fretless instrument, the dissonance could be painful.

Drugs were around, but were generally incidental to the main event, which was drinking. There was some acknowledgement that this was the problem, but there was little intention to do anything about it. Being drunk was part of the show. Our own press releases lauded us as being "semi-alcoholic". "Only a fool breaks the one gallon rule" was Sean's oft-repeated drinking advice at gigs, though nobody really knew if the rule was a minimum or a maximum recommendation. With all the distractions, I wasn't writing songs, which bugged me, rightly. *Where I Belong* was the only one that emerged that year.

"Can't remember my own name or who's my friend or who's my foe
Can't remember where I am or where I'm meant to go"

We stayed sober for a TV appearance on the BBC's *Later With Jools Holland*, which was in its first series, but it didn't improve our fortunes. It was a country special, with kd lang and Loudon Wainwright III in the studio with us. The show was pre-recorded but shot live, and we were urged to ride out any minor fluffs and carry on. In the rehearsals we were on the money, and our songs were greeted with whoops and thumbs-ups from kd's band, who sound checked in the studio without her. When the time came to perform, hours later, I had become jaded and ill at ease, and I conspicuously miscued on guitar at the beginning of *In Tall Buildings*. The producer sympathised with me afterwards and said he had considered calling "cut" on the take there and then. I wished he had, or I had. His commiseration told me too much, and I have never been able to watch the recording back.

Jools was very friendly, very nice; he was genuinely interested in what we were doing and what we were into, and he gave me his phone number and invited me to call him and come round his house to listen to records. I kept his phone number but never rang him, which was silly, but typical of me.

I was more relaxed when we appeared on *Top Of The Pops* to perform our track from the Heavenly *Fred EP*, *Deeply Dippy*. Right Said Fred had a string of big hits, starting with *I'm Too Sexy*. Flowered Up had covered their next hit, *Don't Talk Just Kiss,* for a BBC radio session, and that gave Jeff the idea for a Heavenly EP of covers of the gay, bald, body-builders' songs to raise money for the Terrence Higgins Trust. Saint Etienne did the other song on the record, *I'm Too Sexy*.

Hackett expressed doubts about agreeing to sing the quirky Freds cover on the show. I remember us debating it on the tour van, when word had reached us that Flowered Up had cried off sick, and Saint Etienne, who had recently appeared doing their own hit, had demurred so that we could have a crack. I could see Andy's point; the EP was a bit of a laugh, but it wasn't what we were about. Singing a non-country pop ditty would send out a confusing message and make people less inclined to take us seriously. But how could you turn down an appearance on *Top Of The Pops*? If we had, we should only have regretted it, and the decision would have gone down as another of our Big Mistakes.

So we agreed, and Pep, who usually did our on-stage sound, drove us up to the Hertfordshire studio. DJ Gary Davies introduced us on the show, flanked by Liam from Flowered Up and Sarah Cracknell from Saint Etienne, fluttering her feather boa. Our record had entered the charts at No 26. On stage, we played it for laughs, singing live and miming the instruments. We did a tidy enough job. I had brought in a couple of tap-dancing cowgirls from the Pineapple dance agency (you've got to get a gimmick for *The Pops*) and they shuffled along to my real tap steps that you can hear on the record. It all looked lively enough on screen, but in the studio it was a sterile affair. *Top Of The Pops* had entered its slow post-80s decline, and this was a particularly thin offering. The audience was small in number, only two other acts made personal appearances and the rest of the show was made up of videos.

After the show, Shakespeares Sister were friendly and said hi. They complimented our song and we said we liked theirs, but the former Bananarama plus one showed no interest in joining us for a drink; this was regular work for them, no special occasion. As for The Little Angels, they were nowhere to be seen. In the BBC Elstree Studio bar we recognised Dot Cotton from *Eastenders*, who supposedly spent more time there than in the fictional Queen Vic, but the only people around who had been on our show were a few stray teenage girls from the audience, who we cajoled into coming to sit with us. A few drinks later, three of them accepted a lift back to London to have a nightcap at the Good Mixer. Chris, glorying in the joys of his new-found fame, kept saying "I've gone to heaven". Pep just laughed at our impropriety; he had worked with other bands who easily picked up interest from such very young female admirers, but for us, this was a first. It came to nothing, thank goodness. In the famous Camden rock boozer, our pretty sixth-form acquaintances suddenly went sober on us at the thought of school the next day, and declined proposals to go further on to the Marathon, the aptly-named kebab house that provided after hours beers for Camden's 24-hour party people. The girls phoned their dads to come and rescue them, and before long they were gone. It was a mercy. In truth we were perhaps as far out of our depth as they were. The following week, the EP sank from the charts into pop music oblivion, and our seven days of stardom went with it.

The summer had ended at the Reading Festival with The Rockingbirds Rolling Revue topping the bill on the second stage on Sunday. Our all-star show featured Suggs, Edwyn Collins and Vic Godard along with people from our earlier Rolling Revues: Caroline, Joss, Lesley and Chalky The Yorkie. Our show was heralded with a big spread in the *Melody Maker*. The piece "rumoured" that Kevin Rowland from Dexys might also appear with us, which prompted an even stronger rumour that Kevin was mightily pissed off at the music paper's baseless misinformation. As Reading climaxed on the final night we attracted a few hardcore Rockingbirds enthusiasts but it was only a moderate crowd, as the great mass of festival-goers flocked to see Nirvana making rock history on the main stage.

We carried on doing gigs for the rest of the year. In the autumn we did a run of college dates, but there was little buy-in from the freshmen, who didn't know what to make of us. "Are you wearing fancy dress?" asked a girl at one university, questioning the choice of cowboy boots and shirts that myself and DJ Robin were wearing. We had good followings in some places; gigs at Glasgow's King Tut's Wah Wah Hut, Oxford's Jericho Tavern and the Sheffield Leadmill could be really good. But in other places... not so much.

I have no excuses, it was my fault; I wasn't doing my job, at least partly because I never properly understood that I *had* a job. I thought my work was done; our one album had been made, and I believed our own hype and thought that this was marvellous and fascinating enough. I was wrong. I scorned other bands who I thought "workmanlike", not realising that this was really a job like any other. We were Heavenly: *Believe In Magic* was our motto. But I believed in it all too much. I was hopelessly unworldly, and increasingly distracted from what I needed to be doing, which was playing well and writing songs. It was not so hard, but I had made it so.

The last gig of the year was in a theatre in Sunderland. It was less than half-full. At the end there were a few calls for an encore, and we disagreed about whether to go back on; I hate to go back on if the calls are half-hearted and dwindling. I said to Hackett, if you want to do an encore, go right ahead and sing one yourself. I finished the tour sitting in the front row watching my own band play *Rockin' All Over The World,* with Hackett remembering most, if not all, of the words.

We found Agoristo, in the end, thanks to our pal Annie Nightingale. The BBC DJ had taken a shine to my dream horse story, tracked down the owners of Road To Riches, and took us all out one rainy day to wherever the beast was stabled, out in the shires somewhere, with press in tow. The owners were genteel and welcoming; excited in particular at their BBC celebrity DJ guest. They entertained us generously with luxury nibbles and Chivas

Regal. I enquired about buying the horse, but was kindly warned off such a rash investment; stabling costs were steep, and Road To Riches had taken an injury since his win earlier in the year, and likely would not race again.

The story about The Rockingbirds finding Agoristo never made it to the presses, perhaps because the editor decided it was all a lot of nonsense, probably because it really *was* a lot of nonsense. But I do have a 10x8 photo of The Rockingbirds standing with Road To Riches at his stable door. It may have been a lot of nonsense, but it is all true.

*

Anna and I were set to get wed on the second day of January, 1993. Dave Morgan was my best man. Anna had a red dress made, and I had a green suit off the peg from Kensington Market (an unlucky colour combination, someone later told me). There was no stag do or anything: it was a funny time of year for that, maybe. We spent New Year's Day on our own together, in our flat on Adelaide Road in Chalk Farm, and had an early night of it. I had a bit of a cry, but Anna didn't ask me what was wrong, or get offended, as she might have. She just held on, and so did I. The next day, we got married.

The Blue Man

THREE YEARS AFTER the first Rockingbirds album, the title of our second asked what had become of us country-strumming likely lads, or it would have, had I remembered to add a question mark. Without the correct punctuation, *Whatever Happened To The Rockingbirds* is more a statement than a question. Whatever... Here, briefly, are some answers to that almost-asked question.

We had lost our record deal. Sony dropped us after the first year, following a short and unreassuring extension. Warners followed suit, declining to make any further investment in us when our publishing contract expired after the first year.

1993 saw *Rockingbirds 'R' Us* come out independently on Heavenly. After our wedding my songwriting livened up for a while and I wrote three of the four songs on the EP in a week. The toy shop reference and more dinosaurs on the cover didn't delight everyone in the band, but apart from that, we were pretty satisfied with what we had done. Recorded at Bark, it was a little bit country and a little bit more power pop. The lead track, *Gladly,* pinched words from Alex Chilton, Elvis, Vic Godard and Elvis again, in quick succession:

> *"Did you get my message?*
> *Will you meet me at the pool?*
> *Love me tender, be your age,*
> *Oh baby, don't be cruel"*

The chorus then resolved on a more familiar Rockingbirding theme:

> *"How much did I have last night?*
> *How many is a few?*
> *Gladly I would tell you if I knew"*

The song got some good reviews and then disappeared into the nowhere-realm between pop, indie and country that we had carved out for ourselves. "Number 1 – in a parallel universe", as Hackett would say. The more the joke was repeated, the more hysterically funny it became.

We gigged when we could. Our ban from the acoustic stage at Glastonbury proved to be all wind and air; we were back there in 1993, with an early afternoon slot on the *NME* stage as well, getting us into the backstage VIP area. Here our man Hackett distinguished himself by "snogging" Brett Anderson. The frontman from Suede (that year's big new thing) had recently made his ambivalent sexual orientation known to all, in an interview where he confessed he had yet to go all the way, in a gay way. Spotting him as he came by, our lead guitarist took it upon himself to help him break his duck there and then. Briefly introducing himself with the words "Oi Brett! I'll give you your first homosexual experience – in the van!" He then jumped him and tried to get his tongue past the unconsenting singer's tightly pursed lips. The incident may have earned The Rockingbirds a mention or two in the post-Glastonbury music press gossip, but the gravity of the sexual offence was registered by absolutely nobody.

To Glastonbury we had brought along the whole crew, as we did everywhere else. Integral to our entourage were our merchandising men, who had joined us later in '92. Frank and Briggs from Brighton had built an impressive wooden merch stand painted with cartoon cowgirls and the Rockingbirds logo along the top, and they valiantly touted our T-shirts and other bits and bobs, including the Gradually Learning jigsaw puzzle and the Rockingbirds belt buckle with pointy, metal roses that dinged a hole in the back of my acoustic the one time I wore one.

Sound engineer Pep remained with us. He would go on to work with Saint Etienne when they started gigging in the mid-90s, as did Frank and Briggs and our tour manager, Charlie Browne. Charlie had taken over in 1993 from the previous short-lived incumbent, another unreliable type we had unwisely adopted from the Flowered Up camp. Charlie broke the pattern of incompetence; he was an astute, can-do, dependable dude – a Norfolk good old boy. His Borstal-schooled iron-man qualities later won him his dream job working as Morrissey's batman. Charlie was a huge Moz fan, and the baby Morrissey held on the cover of *Years Of Refusal* is Charlie's kid.

We hired a sleeper van and driver for one tour, to save money on hotels and to enjoy the full '24 hours on the road' lifestyle experience. The driver was a grudging gremlin we nicknamed Spanner, who had driven for Prince as well as numerous well-known British heavy metal acts (or the crews thereof). At the first date at Edward's No. 8 in Birmingham, Spanner came in to the soundcheck to give us a listen. "Not exactly Saxon, are they?" he muttered to our crew. Evidently, he liked Saxon. "*Not exactly Saxon*"; words that will stay with me to my grave, if not on it.

On that tour we had an up-and-coming Scots group supporting us. Whiteout had recorded at Bark, and hoped to sign to Heavenly, but ended up on Silvertone, the Stone Roses' old label. Soon after touring with us, Whiteout went out with another up-and-coming group by the name of Oasis, with the two bands alternating the headline slot each night. I saw them at the 100 Club. I thought Oasis were quite a laugh, rehashing 70s hit tunes like *I'd Like To Teach The World To Sing*. I thought our mates Whiteout were sure to be more successful, another minor misjudgement on my part. A year or so after that we did a tour supporting our friends Dodgy, who were in the Britpop ascendant.

Dave Morgan had gone. He left after a miserable outing at the Fleadh Festival in Finsbury Park in 1993. I had come to the festival directly from an all-nighter at the Leisure Lounge in Holborn with Hackett, and was in a very ragged state, not match-fit. Caroline, in the company of Pete Astor, Sukie Smith and a few other friends, witnessed the sorry spectacle and her report of it shamed her boyfriend into announcing his departure. I learned this from Dave only years later. No doubt there were other reasons, with this the final straw. At the time, when Dave told me he was quitting, I don't remember asking him for a reason, I just said, "OK". My best friend was leaving our band and I didn't even ask him why. I just let it pass before me, with no sense of being able to redirect things or make things better.

We got another drummer, someone Chris knew, Trevor Smith. A remarkably taciturn chap, was Trevor, but a decent guy and an accomplished musician. Joolie the fiddle player was no longer showing up, but we took on another recruit, Tim Kent on banjo, from the London bluegrass band Foghorn Leghorn. Tim was a skilful picker whose bright tones brought the band some much-needed sparkle and zip.

Anna and I split up after an 18-month attempt at married life, and I took up lodgings in gloomy Clapton in north-east London. I was in a house-share with Pep, where he would also share his after-the-pub bottle of Valpolicella with me, which I partly paid him back for by losing small sums to him at backgammon each night.

Why did Anna and I split up? Just selfish, frivolous things, certainly on my part. Like... I would get annoyed with her for taking too long to get herself ready of an evening. What is the point of not leaving the flat till after 10 when the pubs close at 11? Once I was gone, Anna came into her own, and she and our raven-haired Scottish pal Jackie made a name for themselves as quite the weekend party girls, taking just as long as they liked in the evenings to get dolled up and staying out all night at clubs like Blow Up, The Frat Shack and other modish retro haunts. That showed me.

Before we split up, Anna and I had tried to buy a place together. I had money in the bank for a deposit, she had a job. It should have been easy but I was a poll tax refusenik which meant I hadn't been on the electoral roll for a few years. The building society couldn't run a credit check, and I was taken aback when the stern woman from the Nationwide rebuked me for not paying my taxes and declined our mortgage application.

I learned later there were other routes for uncreditworthy but temporarily cash-rich musicians like me to get mortgages. Things might have been different (security, shared responsibility, kids?), but I was easily steered off the straight and narrow. My unworldly, socialistic aversion to property ownership also came into it, directing me to an unsettled life of serial renting.

Mike Stewart had been making regular trips from Austin and he helped us record a demo. We were interested in recording with old-school valve equipment, in keeping with the band's preference for old guitars and amplification. It was around this time Andy Hackett started his vintage guitar trading business at the pawnbroker's in the Angel, Islington. Liam Watson's Toe Rag Studios had opened in Shoreditch, and Edwyn Collins was getting a studio together too, similarly embracing valve values. We did our demo at Chiswick Reach, another retrograde recording house. The proprietor looked the part in his lab coat and all, but the place was a work in progress. Mike confessed afterwards he was driven nearly to despair trying to get sufficient channels to work through the desk.

I wanted Mike to be our manager, but he was unsure. Obviously we needed one, we always had, but the right person never presented themselves. Mike went to see none other than former Pink Floyd manager Peter Jenner, who ran Sincere Management, a company based in West London. We met and Peter agreed to take us on, assigning a young sidekick to look after us. The first thing they suggested was we do a tour with Hank Wangford, another of the acts they managed. Hank became a good friend in years to come, but at that time, I confess, I didn't think doing a tour with him on the UK folk circuit would be a good look, credibility-wise. The Peter Jenner situation fizzled out; we were not to be managed.

We wanted Edwyn Collins to produce us in his new studio. I had been a fan of Orange Juice in the early Postcard Records days, and though my interest had dwindled in the 80s, it was restored by Piece Thompson who got me into Edwyn's solo record *Hope And Despair,* which had countrified tracks like *Putting It To The Back Of My Mind.* It was a great album, Hackett concurred. We would go to every Edwyn gig we could and would do our best to chat him up, one way or another. Hackett had already done some groundwork on this back in Norwich, where he had promoted a late-period Orange Juice gig. These efforts to court our favourite Scottish balladeer culminated in us getting him on board for our Reading Rockingbirds Rolling Revue in '92, and Andy and Edwyn became close friends. Early on, Ed would quake "Oh no! Not Andrew Hackett," peeping through the outstretched fingers of his face-palm in faux terror at the mere mention of his name, but he loved him really.

Grace Maxwell, Edwyn's wife and manager, was offering us a good deal on the studio – or she would, when it was ready. We would be their guinea pigs, the first to use it. But we still needed a record deal to fund the recording and put the record out. Eventually an unlikely arrangement was reached between Jeff at Heavenly and Martin Goldschmidt at Cooking Vinyl, an unfashionable but thriving independent at the more rootsy end of the label spectrum. Goldschmidt wanted the Heavenly name and logo on the record, to lend the release a bit of Heavenly hipness, but in reality it was a Cooking Vinyl record.

Once Edwyn and his engineer Sebastian Lewsley had installed the 70s Neve desk in their premises in Alexandra Palace, North London, we were ready to go. By now it was 1995, and all our personal financial gains from The Rockingbirds' major deals had evaporated, with only looming income tax bills left to trouble us. Edwyn and Grace were also hard up, having sunk all they had into the studio. Grace drove an old banger and they had a cheerless one-bedroom flat in Kilburn, which also accommodated their wee son William, with his toddler toys strewn about. When we started recording, I remember us all bunking our fares at Alexandra Palace station, Edwyn included.

New River studio was named after the adjacent man-made watercourse, and recording there was a lot of fun. Edwyn and Seb's in-studio comedy alter-egos were later preserved in the characters of Denny Lorimer and Jackson Gold in their wilfully atrocious Channel 4 flop sitcom, *West Heath Yard,* which also starred Andy Hackett and the Sex Pistols' Paul Cook in the roles of rock wannabes. There were a few early technical hitches at New River, which kept the band waiting in the Starting Gate pub on the first day, with predictable results, but after that things went smoothly. After a couple of weeks, Texas Mike came by and we got a mix up of the album's longest track, *I Woke Up One Morning*, which sounded swell.

But when we started to get the mixes home, Andy and I were less than happy. They just didn't sound that good – not terrible, but not tip-top, not crystal, a bit distorted and muffled, lacking in the oomph you would expect from a modern, hi-fidelity recording. It was hard to describe it, exactly. Andy and I took the mixes round to Edwyn and Grace's to see what they had to say. We A-B-ed the recordings with other recordings, but they were not convinced there was anything wanting or wrong. It was all rather unsatisfactory and inconclusive... and embarrassing! What we thought we could hear, or not hear, they were not perceiving, or in denial about; it was all in the ear of the beholder, perhaps, my old "same sense data, different perception" conundrum, once again. In the end, we yielded to their expertise and settled with what we had. What else could we do? We recorded a couple of other tracks, *Band*

Of Dreams and *Roll On Forever,* at Bark, which I had greater confidence in.

When we were done, Edwyn began recording his own album, *Gorgeous George,* at the studio, with Sean contributing backing vocals. After they started, something stopped working, a faulty amplifier of some kind was replaced, and after that everything sounded way better. Or, at least, so I heard. The single from the album, *A Girl Like You,* was a huge hit all around the world, and Edwyn and Grace's fortunes were transformed. It must have sold millions, but if they hadn't sorted out that amp, well... I suspect it might have sold many thousands fewer.

The cover of *Whatever Happened...* has us (sans drummer and banjo player) gathered around a log on Hampstead Heath in front of a big blue sky. I now liked country album covers with big blue skies. In contrast, on the back was a picture of a dead condor hanging by its feet from a rope, with an Andean cowboy below it punching upwards. The photograph was cropped from a gruesome article about ritual vulture-hunting in Peru that I had found in *National Geographic* magazine. Was I trying to make some kind of point about how cruel the world could be to us birds? That might have been the idea. If I had, I might have struggled to explain who or what had been so unkind to us.

The album starts brightly with *Roll On Forever,* which is a good country song, well recorded. *I Like Winter* follows with a jaunty banjo mood and a quirky, contrarian sentiment, but we thought it a little in the mud, soundwise – as we did the next track, *Everybody Lives With Us,* another decent tune, the one Edwyn liked best. *Band Of Dreams* is an autobiographical number that we released as a single. It referenced some on-tour misadventures and anticipated our demise:

> *"One time in a foreign land*
> *It got a little out of hand*
> *And a few times our support band*

> *Were the only ones who showed*
> *I don't like excuses*
> *But old clichés have their uses*
> *'Cos it's a very hard place to write songs on the road"*

Finishing off the first side, we continued to feel a little sad for ourselves by covering Troy Seals and Donnie Fritts' *We Had It All*.

The album has its merits and admirers, and though Andy and I had grumbled about the sound, nobody outside the band ever did. It had bright moments, but the mood overall was downbeat. Those who had criticised us before for being "eager to please" were not now rushing to applaud us for grappling with darker themes.

Hell, on side two, was Frank and Briggs' favourite track; a surprising preference, I thought. It was fast and furious, it had that going for it, but it employed Jean-Paul Sartre's most famous quote, and the message was a tad bleak:

> *"Hell is other people*
> *Hell is in your mind*
> *When hope is what you're looking for*
> *Hell is what you'll find"*

After we did a live acoustic performance on London radio station GLR, the production team looked for an upbeat tune from our new album to play after we'd made our appearance, and went for *Hell*. They swiftly took it off the afternoon airwaves as it came to the conclusion of the first chorus:

> *"Hell is in the wintertime*
> *Hell is in the spring*
> *Hell's in every fucking little thing"*

*

You don't know what you've got till it's gone, goes the song. We hadn't achieved the success we or others had hoped for, but we still had fans and people out there rooting for us. The *R'Us* EP record sleeve invited people to contact us via *Truckers Wives*, c/o the

Heavenly address, 72 Wardour Street, and people wrote, lots of them. To my shame, I did a poor job of replying, and many letters, maybe a hundred of them, lay in a pile unanswered.

One reply that I did make brought unpleasant consequences. The initial letter I received, which I picked up at the Heavenly office, asked something about Gram Parsons. The questions seemed lame and gauche to me and I dashed off a flippant response. Anna was with me at the time, saw what I had written, and told me not to be horrible and not to send it, but in stupid defiance, I sent it. The next time I was in the office, a few days later, Martin Kelly fielded a telephone call – someone was asking for me. He listened and then started apologising, and I soon twigged that this was the person I had sent my shitty letter to, who was ringing the office to try to give me, or someone, a piece of his mind. I quickly made myself scarce, as Martin held the telephone receiver an arm's length away from his ear.

This sort of thing on my part, taking fans for granted, or worse, for fools, is not something I will dignify by trying to explain. Any explanation you care to speculate on is likely to have some truth in it, I expect. Clearly some destructive impulse was at play. These are my confessions, after all, not my excuses, and though I affect to be honest in this book, my biggest confession may be that there are some things I am not going to be fool enough to admit to. This is the saddest part of my story, and I am trying to make this chapter as short as I can.

Our second album had done something, but not enough. Hackett met up with me in the Engine Room in Camden to tell me Sean wanted out of the band, and if Sean was going, he wanted out too. I said that in that case there was no point in the group going on at all, so we should call an end to the whole damned thing. As with Dave's departure, it all seemed an inevitable unravelling, and not something I wanted to fight against. Sean was in demand with other musicians, Lawrence, Edwyn and now Beth Orton. Dave

Morgan came back to join us for the farewell gig at The Garage in November 1995, Sean put all his cowboy shirts on the Rockingbirds merchandise stand, and others in the band did the same. At the end of the night, Pep took the merch stand and made a bed out of it in his lockup in Hackney, where he was now living.

Before that final gig, I had bumped into Nikki Sudden at Dingwalls. Don't quit the band, was his unasked-for advice. Carry on as The Rockingbirds, with whoever you can get to do it with you. People will respect you for it. He spoke from his perhaps bitter post-Swell Maps experience. He was right. I sort of knew even then that Nikki was right, but it was all decided, and all agreed, and the farewell gig had been advertised and the tickets were sold. We just had to act out our roles in the story, and move on.

It was like David Byrne had famously said, "People will remember you better if you always wear the same outfit".

*

But the desire to adopt a new identity was strong. One good reason to leave The Rockingbirds was so I could do something new with Sean, who had initiated the split. The new thing was to be Famous Times, which, in essence, was just me and Sean, collaborating with whoever we wanted, something other acts like Massive Attack had done. I got our name from a Richard Ford short story that appeared in Granta. *Rock Springs* is about a small-time dude who steals a car and sets off with his girlfriend to start a new life. Before they leave he gets a tattoo on his arm saying FAMOUS TIMES. I got a tattoo just the same, with a cross, an anchor and a heart – faith, hope and charity.

Jeff Barrett was still backing us. He and Martin Kelly got us a publishing deal, a 'development deal' with Heavenly Songs, backed by Phonogram. It was not a big deal, it probably was not even a good deal, but it gave us an advance to share between ourselves, and keep us going. We'd be a songwriting partnership this time, with everything credited to Tyler/Read, like Lennon/McCartney or Nanker/Phelge. On the contract we were asked to write down the titles of our new songs to be published. We managed to muster 10, I think, including one Sean wrote on his own, *Lighthouse Keeper*.

In practice there was little genuine co-writing. On *The Big O* we both contributed separate sections, but on other songs it was me writing the words, chords and melody ('*Keeper* excepted), and then Sean making his considerable contributions with the arrangements. I have never been much for co-composing. Sitting in a room together, and bashing something out; it's never worked for me, so far… it's too embarrassing: I don't think I can do it if someone else is watching.

In the Rockingbirds, Andy Hackett would sometimes share a guitar bit he had come up with, but I would never run with it, perhaps to his frustration. I was open to ideas, but these were not the ideas that interested me. My songwriting approach put lyrics before music. If I had some words, or even just an inspiring song title, then I could build a song, but some chords and a riff? That was not what usually sparked the process, for me.

Was I being obstructive, wanting to keep the control and the songwriting glory for myself? Possibly, in some subtle or not so subtle way, I might have put the others off, but not intentionally, because we always wanted new songs. Writing was never easy, never 'natural', always some kind of struggle, and each one in the bag felt like it might be my last. I never felt confident or complacent about whatever talent I had, which may have been a weakness, but it may have lent a strength and urgency to what did come through. If someone in the band had eased my burden and presented a song of their own then I would likely have welcomed it, but there was no "voila!" moment from any other Rockingbird, so I remained our lone 'content provider'.

Big Steve Tree was someone who could write a number, and he had a corker that I was happy to take a back seat on. The first

Famous Times record was a Heavenly 7" with Big Steve singing *Springboard* on one side, and our song, *Something To Believe*, on the other. After that, we assembled at Edwyn's upgraded studio in West Heath Yard, West Hampstead to do more recording, with Big Steve on guitar and vocals and the old gang on drums and bass, Dave Morgan and Chris Clarke.

Out of this came the *Blue Man EP*. *The Blue Man* is one of my best songs, and at 5:41 it is certainly one of the longest. The arrangement on record takes its time to get going: it might have been better to have scrapped the intro and gone straight in on the vocal. But from the verse onwards the song's three-section construction builds interestingly and effectively, with lush, Carpenters-esque backing vocals on the choruses, and tremendous horns and strings arranged by Sean (especially the stirring final instrumental section, which somebody should use on the TV for something, sometime). Martin Kelly did his best to get the song to Neil Diamond. We liked that idea, but nothing gave. When the song is released from its 30-year publishing deal handcuffs, I mean to get my present publishers to give it another push, and get a star to sing it. Someone big.

The few people who heard the record liked it, but we had gone further into that big black hole where Planet Rockingbird existed in its parallel universe. There was no genuine expectation of success, and it felt like we were an indulgence for Heavenly, which in the end won't do. At a certain point, Jeff phoned me to let me know that the album deal that he had been promising now could not be. That was quite a tough one, that night, sitting in dreary Clapton with a black and white portable TV for company and whatever it was I had to drink. The Famous Times were at an end.

It had been getting difficult to get anything together with Sean, anyway. Though we were officially in a band together, he was busy with Beth Orton, recording and touring, and I didn't want to get in the way of that, even if I did have a kind of claim on him, partnership-wise. The following year, I was given notice by Phonogram that the publishing deal was expiring; there would be no further advance of cash. I called Sean to give him the bad but hardly unexpected news, but it turned out it was only I who was being dropped; they were keeping Sean, whose co-writes with Beth were bringing in some actual returns on their advance.

Wow! Well, that was good news, for Sean. Me? I was The Blue Man. Out in the cold... out on the ice.

In Tall Buildings

CHALKY THE YORKIE was singing my praises. "Al, you've written some good tunes, you really have... lovely lyrics... but the one I like best is... ooh, what's it called now?" He paused to think for a moment before it came to him. "*Tall Buildings*, that's the one! Aaah, that's a cracker, that is."

In Tall Buildings, written by John Hartford, is a tender country waltz which has been sung by many artists, including The Rockingbirds. The song is a lament for a dude who gives up on his dreams and hippy ideals, buys a suit, cuts off his hair, and gets a straight job working in an office.

I suppose if I was not to walk into the Texas desert to disappear into the lost land of Agoristo, living out the lyrics of this song was a more achievable outcome, and perhaps something I had always half anticipated. If Famous Times were not to be, I was not too proud to settle for some quieter days of obscurity directed by some employer or other. As it has turned out, though my public profile has not ascended, I have been more musically productive in my last 20 or so years of being occupied with 'proper jobs' than I had been in the similar length of time before that.

Describing the job I got in 1997 as "proper" would, admittedly, be a stretch. Speedex News was a media monitoring firm, working from a couple of rooms at 32 Paddington Street, just above the shops. Their business name resembled Tellex News, their more legitimate media-monitoring rival. Speedex was the bandit version of Tellex. They didn't have clients on a formally-contracted basis, as Tellex had, they just fired out pirated tapes and the odd transcript to anyone they thought might pay the carbon-copied invoices which we wrote out by hand and sent with them.

With not a computer in sight, along one side of the office were shelves of small television sets hooked up to VHS machines. These were cheap domestic appliances anyone might buy, recording anything of any conceivable interest. We targeted news, fashion and 'lifestyle' programmes that mentioned public bodies, businesses, fashion designers and retail outlets; any concern that might have a PR or press office that might pay to learn about their media coverage. My job was to watch the targeted programmes, log content, and when a company or organisation was mentioned, to ring up their press office and sell them a videotape copy of their moment on air, priced at £35 per clip, plus VAT.

Sat at his desk just next to the bank of TVs was the proprietor, Peter Johnson, a large Indian man whose real name was Vidya Anand. He watched over everything like a great bird of prey, constantly on the lookout for mentions of our paying customers. Debenhams was one of the foremost among these. Whenever he caught a mention of Debenhams by Lorraine Kelly on *GMTV* or on Richard and Judy he would cry out "DEBENHAMS!" in triumph, instruct one of his minions to "make tape" and sit back in his extravagant ergonomic chair with a purr of satisfaction.

Peter presided over the office on weekdays from eight-thirty in the morning until the early evening TV news came on at six. Speedex News media monitoring was a demanding business, but he allowed himself some light relief by watching *The Jerry Springer Show* each afternoon, a programme he had taken an intense liking to despite it having no economic value to him whatsoever. Viewing it on the TV screen next to his desk and listening with headphones, the spectacle of low-status Americans confecting domestic conflict for the TV cameras delighted our boss beyond reason, and as we toiled on the telephones to get any last sales before home-time, he provided us with vocal commentary on the more dramatic moments, sometimes pointing and squealing with delight, "...she is *shouting* at him and *pulling* her hair... and he tried to *HIT* him... Oh God, it's so great. So funny!" Jerry Springer never failed to please our Peter.

His one notable absence from work was when he went on a trip to China and the Middle East for a number of weeks that September. Aside from his commitment to his beloved Speedex, the other Peter, the writer Vidya Sagar Anand, was a man of substance and status in India and on the world stage. A historian and poet in his native Urdu, he also cultivated certain political connections and aspirations. His book, *In Search of Dr. Sun Yat-Sen, Father Of Modern China*, which was published in 1999 by the impressively named Institute of Media Communications (address: 32 Paddington Street, London W1) enlightens us about his 1997 Chinese "pilgrimage". Following the publication of his previous book *The Prisoner Of Portland Place* in 1996, Vidya had been invited by the Chinese People's Political Consultative Conference (CPPCC) to give a lecture in Beijing on their post-imperial President Sun Yat-Sen, the revolutionary predecessor of Chairman Mao. This lecture (along with two others delivered in London, all contained in the book) described and commemorated the events of 100 years before, when the future Chinese leader had been kidnapped on a London street and imprisoned at the Chinese Legation in Portland Place by his own country's imperial authorities. I had, I must admit, no knowledge of Sun Yat-Sen, prior to reading all this, despite my familiarity with that locale.

Vidya's speech to his Chinese comrades paid hagiographic homage to the venerable Sun. The socialist who had freed his country from the yoke of feudalism was "one of your greatest sons", he said, and he saluted "the people of modern China... the sole source of light for the overwhelming majority, the developing and struggling mass of humanity." His book also welcomed "the creation of a multipolar world, eschewing superpower hegemony," and in return the Chinese Ambassador to the UK expressed his "warm congratulations and sincere appreciation" for Vidya's work in his book's foreword. A similar contribution from The Rt Hon Tony Benn MP welcomed my employer's positive contribution to our understanding of modern China.

So Speedex was not only Peter's place of business, it was Vidya's eagle's eyrie from which he surveyed the world's shifting geopolitical scene. He was swift to defend General Gaddafi whenever he appeared on the news. The Libyan leader had given Vidya a personal audience on his way back from China. Gaddafi was a great man, much maligned and misunderstood, he assured us; the thing about him farting all the time was a western media lie.

One day in the office, instead of shouting "DEBENHAMS!" he shouted "BIN LADEN!" We monitored CNN, who had an exclusive on the al-Qaeda leader. Their journalist had tracked him down and interviewed him in his Afghan mountain hideaway. Bin Laden had declared jihad against the west, and other news channels were picking up the story. The Royal Embassy of Saudi Arabia was, somehow, one of our significant customers. "Saudis will buy. Two tapes of everything. Transcripts of everything," he ordered with great excitement. I had never heard of Osama Bin Laden until that day; Vidya knew.

Other characters on the firm included Mr Malik. A patient, lugubrious character, "Malik Sahib'" looked after the money and spent much of his time on the phone trying to sweet-talk the ladies of the accounts departments into paying our invoices. Then there was Krishnan, a dark-skinned Indian of a humbler caste who did odd jobs in exchange for using the office as a base for his dubious business ventures, one of which involved reviving the old Iraqi dinar and selling it back to the sanctions-starved Iraqis – something along those lines, anyway. A similar-sounding criminal caper was later exposed in *Private Eye*. Arrests had been made, but the name of Krishnan thankfully did not appear; perhaps our colleague was just one of the scheme's foolhardy investors. Krishnan also had political ambitions and with Vidya's blessing he took a punt on joining the fledgling UK Independence Party (UKIP), and stood, unsuccessfully of course, as a candidate. His wife was a dancer, he told us, a very beautiful dancer at one time, of some renown in his community. "But she is old bag now," he added abruptly, as if desiring to be as colloquially misogynistic as any other Englishman.

The company monitored radio broadcasts as well as TV, and this was attended to mainly by Alistair, a well-spoken chap who had presumably once benefited from an elite public school education but appeared to have made nothing of his advantages, and was sadly negligent in his dress and grooming. Malik's plan to gather our tax details and put us on PAYE alarmed poor Alistair, who protested that he had never had a National Insurance number, and it was too late for him to get one now. Ayako was a young Japanese woman who came in to monitor the evening TV. Ayako was very stern and would not talk to anyone, especially if they were a man, which unfortunately we all were. It turned out that in real life Ayako was a gig-going indie kid who liked Jonathan Richman and was a fan of Comet Gain, some of whom had been early fans of The Rockingbirds. She knew who I was, but never said. It was Piers

Miller, my musician friend, who found this out; he worked at Speedex too.

*

A sure way to avoid significant success is to maintain modest aspirations, something I have always been true to when it comes to finding a home. I may have fecklessly blown my chance for home ownership, but with luck and resourcefulness I have done quite well at finding cheap and interesting places to rent in London. The clichéd aspiration of a rock star would be a mansion in Virginia Water or a crumbling castle in Spain. Ordinary mortals feed their acquisitive fancies watching TV programmes like *Homes Under The Hammer,* which I find ghastly. My humble but no less romantic hope was always to live, Quentin Crisp-like, in some insalubrious but well-located lodging in the beating heart of London town.

Happily, this wish was achieved and even exceeded, early in 1999. Genuinely affordable council and housing association rents were almost impossible to find by the late 90s, but I had heard of a housing provider that still accepted self-referrals from the public on one day of the year. My girlfriend and I rang them up to find out when this day was to be, and I left a message on their answering machine. It turned out that we had called on the very day their list was opened. At the end of a lengthy application process we were offered, and accepted, a low-rent, two-bedroom flat in Covent Garden, London WC2.

It was a marvellous stroke of good fortune; I was delighted, we both were. I called it my civic inheritance. The flat was on the top floor, and with no lift it was deemed unsuitable to let to a family, and allocated to us. Nature abhorring a vacuum, the spare bedroom was soon to find an occupant. Before the millennium was out we had a baby daughter, and all had come right with the world. Five years from then we were to separate, sadly, and I would have to maintain my cherished commitment to fatherhood living in other places and under more strained circumstances. But back then it was a joyful time and a new start in life, and I loved our darling daughter Christina as I do now, forever and always.

Shakespeare wrote of the seven ages of man. By a more simple minded reckoning, I count five stages of life, with parenthood the third, following childhood and young adulthood. That second stage I had hung on to for 20 years, according to the modern trend. I never aspired to be a dad, but I think becoming one was good for me. Now, with little C grown up and making her own way, I am at my life's fourth stage, the post-parental one. It's a bittersweet time; you are not the all-important person to your offspring that you once were, but you have time for reflection, a time to consolidate or make good, if you can, as your fifth and final phase looms up... old age, ill-health, incapacity and dependency all becoming likelier as you get towards the end, according to your luck.

*

There was a bust-up at Speedex News, and I stopped going in. They allowed me to log the BBC Breakfast news for them at home, and I did the odd transcript that I faxed or emailed from my iMac. On one of my regular visits to Chadwick Street Jobcentre in Victoria I saw a local job advertised for an Administrative Assistant in the Department for Education & Skills, based in their smart new offices at Sanctuary Buildings, Great Smith Street. The job was offered under the Labour New Deal employment scheme. I applied for it and got it, and started working at the lowest civil service rank in the Private Office Business Team, providing admin services to the Secretary of State for Education, Estelle Morris, and all her ministers. This was at the beginning of 2001.

Going to work in tall buildings, I was reverting to a type set by my dad. When young, parents and children see mainly their differences, but as you get older, your similarities become more evident; sometimes startlingly so.

Stricken with TB and hospitalised for a long period as a young man, Dad's modest ambition to train to be a physiotherapist after school at 16 had been scuppered. When he had recovered and served his two years of national service in the Royal Army Medical Corps, he found employment as a bookkeeper, and when I was little he worked in accounts at the Frigidaire factory in Burnt Oak, northwest London.

As he advanced into old age I tried to tap him for snippets from his past that he never cared to speak of before. One thing was, a teacher at Hendon Grammar had said on his report he was "one not likely to be a leader of men". We laughed at this priggish indictment, but our amusement masked a small shared pain. As a child, I was no likely leader of men either, or of boys, girls or anyone else. In the civil service, no-one was to spot in me the leadership qualities required for advancement through the ranks. Dad was always similarly passed over at work; a lack of guile, being "a simple soul", as he would self-knowingly put it, didn't help him, and being a shop steward for the ASTMS union probably didn't help either.

But in my country music-making realm in north London, which more than anything else now focused around my long-running live music event called Come Down & Meet The Folks, I have become something of a leader, somehow. When Folks friends sometimes call me "Sir Alan" or even "Our Leader" it is meant, of course, lightly and in jest, but still, it *is* meant. So where (if I may borrow a phrase from John Otway) did I go right?

The Folks started in 1996 at the Engine Room, the bar opposite the Roundhouse in Chalk Farm, Camden where Hackett and I had called time on The Rockingbirds the previous year. It was run by a young Irish couple, Andy and Jacquie, who had papered the walls of the old Belmont pub with pictures and pages from old music papers and magazines. Attracted by the rockin' vibe of the new Camden bar, Food Records boss Andy Ross hosted a fairly high-functioning pop quiz there, which attracted sections of the London rockerati; journos, musos, A&Rs, record shop geeks and, sometimes, Morrissey. I used to play pool there with my old buddy Rex, who put me up in his nearby council flat a couple of times.

By now the old pub trading laws had been abolished, and they could stay open all afternoon on a Sunday. The Engine Room wanted to take full advantage, and Andy was looking for a free music session to bring in a crowd, like the one Irish folk singer Ron Kavana did in a pub down the road. He let my Scottish pal Craig put on a one-day charity event, and I was one of the people who played at it. Back then I didn't like to play solo, but I hit a sweet spot that afternoon that struck the heart (or something) of a cute French mademoiselle, who discreetly proffered me her telephone number before I left. It was a flattering proposal, but one I neglected to follow up. More relevantly, the landlord also had designs on me; he asked me to run a Sunday afternoon music session for him, with a £50 fee and free beer as the necessary inducement. This offer I accepted with no hesitation.

Sean and I were still doing Famous Times, so I roped him in. We sang our songs, played our favourite records on the pub's Technics decks, and found another act to headline every week. The clientele were people we knew from the Camden scene, or what remained of it – people from the Falcon, quite a few from the rocking scene, the retro Frat Shack scene. The remarkably tireless Anna and Jackie came without fail, to round off their weekends.

After a while Sean and I tired of DJing (or people began to tire of us) so others stepped in. Ski was one, then there was French Philippe Migrenne, Tony Two Eyes, Wayne Northern and sometimes Joss Hutton. As far as the acts were concerned, we wanted to keep it country, but there were not many country acts about. DM Bob & The Deficits, The MPE Band, banjo Tim's Foghorn Leghorn, and The Blazing Homesteads were some names we attracted – it was the more off-beam, alternative types that came our way. After those we settled for bluesier acts, the delightfully-named Pimp was one; God knows who else, it was a long time ago, and people I've asked have forgotten. Everyone who was there remembers The Gourds, though. Texas Mike managed them in Austin, and they came over and played for us a couple of times. They slayed us with their now-famous version of Snoop's *Gin And Juice,* and encored with excerpts from *Tommy* – an amazing gig.

As I say, a lot is now lost to the mists. I remember it being a lot of fun though, and full-on. We started at 2pm in those early days, and our gig was over by seven. But then it was on to Big Steve's Big Night Out at Jacksons Lane Arts Centre in Highgate, which was also held every Sunday; more bands, more records, more drinking. And if that was not enough for you, there was always the kebab shop in Highgate Road, which provided an after-show session space and bottles of the dreaded Keo lager for us over-committed revellers.

After a year or two the Engine Room closed down, and Big Steve's Big Night Out had come to an end as well, but this was not the end of Come Down & Meet The Folks... it was just the beginning. The Eagle pub on Camden Road had become Rosie O'Grady's, now run by Sue McKenna, who used to have Spider Stacy staying up there with her, when he wasn't on the road with the Pogues or the Popes. Our food photographer friend Tim Hill lived opposite; he and Big Steve were in Rosie's a lot. Sue would pay a band £200 a gig; the hard-drinking Other Brothers were one of them, Bap Kennedy and Big Steve's new band The Arlenes were others. Steve suggested to Sue that he and I join forces and start a new Come Down & Meet The Folks there, and off we went.

From then on the Folks was set fair for the years and decades to come. Always on a Sunday afternoon, it was free to get in. A DJ would start things up, fairly quietly at first, to keep things convivial, pushing the volume up after all the acts had gone on. Steve and I would jointly host and play songs of our own, then we'd allow a few floor spots where anyone could play. An advertised headline act would come on later, and during their set we would put the pot round, with all the money collected going to the band. They also got some of the £200 from the pub, the rest of which went to pay ourselves and the DJ. It was free and easy; nobody made a fortune but everyone was happy, including the landlady, who enjoyed a busy Sunday afternoon and evening with a friendly crowd when it would otherwise have been quiet.

The Folks became a regular social for a lot of people, and took on a life of its own. It was somewhere for all our friends to gravitate to, and there was an open door for new people to get involved and join in on the small but growing scene. Our country music remit had wide parameters which acknowledged and admitted southern soul, R&B, folk, blues and good old pub rock, which in effect we were reviving in its heartland, with the old 70s pub rock venues like the Tally Ho just up the road.

If I remember a few names of our regular Folks friends from the Rosie's days, I know I risk offending many I fail to include, but no-one will begrudge my mentioning cuddly Lloyd Coombes, MBE ("the big hello and the long goodbye"), who usually brought along his Islington Council colleague, Andy Washington, who later became a tour manager. West Ham fan Ali Rawlings and her mate Liz were invariably on parade, as were troubadour Tom Horne, guitarist and former male model Tom Bowen, and all the other Rock Rangers, who included Rob Brookes, the Rockingbirds' DJ. Photographers Neville Elder and Paddy Doherty were also on the register, as was folk historian Doc Rowe. You can add to these anyone else mentioned earlier with a plausible local connection, and you have made a start on the who's who of Come Down & Meet The Folks.

There was never really any trouble at the Folks; a few regulars grumbled about us invading their quiet pub sometimes, but that was all part of the caper. When Sue left Rosie's and we moved to the rougher Golden Lion in nearby Royal College Street, wide-eyed Sandy in her eccentric tailored outfits danced about delightedly or rudely heckled to make plain her feelings about each act. Unfortunately she had little patience with the sad, slow songs often favoured by singer-songwriters. She may sometimes have had a point about that, but her rude interjections were still an embarrassment. On the whole we put up with her and made a joke of it, though some acts were justifiably put out, Mike Daly from Whiskeytown being the most notable of these. It never got out of hand, though. The landlady at that grand old Victorian pub, Mary Murphy, kept an eye on things and looked after us all.

With gigs every week, remembering all the performers is hard. Emily Barker and the very young Kitty, Daisy & Lewis are two acts that made their debuts at the Golden Lion and went on to build professional careers. Scottish country man John Miller from the Radio Sweethearts played a few times, and his adorable Shoeshine labelmate Laura Cantrell also appeared. Chineseburn, with our multi-instrumentalist friend Tom Hodges playing musical saw, we booked often. An acoustic three-piece called Stagecoach we liked, and they went on to be more successful than I realised, not generally paying attention to such things.

It wasn't all country. There was a triumvirate of blues and R&B artists that we could rely on to pack a crowd and put on a great show: James Hunter (aka Howlin' Wilf), Little George Sueref, and Big Joe Louis. Nikki Sudden played a couple of times, and his friend and fellow Bolan-fanboy Boz Boorer would happily play for us when he was not on the road with Morrissey. Boz and his wife Lynn did the Christmas gig in 2002, and brought Adam Ant along to join the festivities; Adam looked great and performed a version of Elvis's *In The Ghetto*, but seemed a little distracted. We didn't realise he was packing heat – well, a starting pistol – which he pulled later that night at the Prince Of Wales in Kentish Town, getting him into all kinds of trouble.

A new DJ friend of ours I dubbed Jon The Boatman. Jonathan Miller was a handsome old teddy boy with what people used to call a lantern jaw. His live-aboard boat was moored not far from his beloved Wenlock Arms in Islington, where we frequently went to join him to enjoy "the best ale in London", greatly superior to the poor beer he had to endure at the Folks. Jon was a man of firm convictions and sweeping generalisations, which I was always keen to encourage. Elvis was The King (of course), but just below him Jon recognized another regal tier which included Little Richard (the King of Rock'n'roll) Charlie Feathers (King of Rockabilly) and Crazy Cavan, the King of the Teds. The three greatest men of the 20th century (Jon and I decided, after a brisk deliberation) were Elvis Presley, Muhammad Ali, and George Best, and we also agreed that no great music was made after the 70s (apart from the music we put on at our pub, of course).

Other DJs around that time included Honky Tonkin' Tina Ogle (who carried on at the Golden Lion with Honky Tonkin' Sunday after we left), Helen Keen, Pete Bridgeman, DJ Mule Freedom (aka Gerry Ranson), Nick West of music mag *Bucketfull of Brains*, a dodgy Aussie with a huge country collection called Chris, and The Nine Stone Cowboy, aka Irish, real name Plunket McShane. Plunket would sometimes take issue with DJs whose selections strayed too far from the country road. I encouraged him with this admirable work by officially appointing him the Folks' DJ foreman, with the job of keeping the others in line. Plunket remains in post to this day.

We left the Golden Lion to follow Rosie's Sue to the Fiddler's Elbow. The new venue was better set up for gigs; it even had a stage. Once upon a time, when it was the Mother Shipton, it had been a proper fighting pub. I know this because my dad lived opposite as a boy and used to watch from his window as the drunks tipped out onto Malden Crescent on Saturday nights. The pub was on the edge of the Queen's Crescent estate, a working-class enclave like Somers Town in King's Cross, from which many residents rarely strayed. We didn't attract too much trouble; a few things got thrown at us when we stood outside in the summertime... just a few potatoes, that was all. Memorable gigs? I took a chance on left-field Americanos Okkervil River; I liked them but Hackett dissented, and put a pot round while they played to get them to stop (it didn't work, fortunately). Townes Van Zandt's reclusive son, John Townes Van Zandt II, did a beautiful solo show. Some of my own gigs went well. Many good times.

*

At some point around the end of the 20th century I had fallen in love with Waylon Jennings. I had seen him at Wembley with The Highwaymen, but at that time he was my least favourite of the four, well behind Willie Nelson, Kris Kristofferson and Johnny Cash. After that I "got him", as people say, and once it clicked I made him my favourite. I particularly loved the funky studio grooves and stuttering Telecaster abstractions characteristic of his records around the 70s. Even my girlfriend liked him, and I remember us skanking around the Covent Garden flat to *Ramblin' Man*. At her suggestion I started a tribute band called Nowaylon, punning on the well-known Oasis apers No Way Sis. My girlfriend may have been taking the mickey, but I took the idea seriously, for a while. The problem was, I couldn't play guitar like Waylon, and neither could anyone else, so the idea fell at the first hurdle. The second hurdle would have been that Waylon's fandom was nowhere big enough to merit a tribute band, but we never got that far.

The Folks gave me a place to play every week, and I was writing songs again. It was at Rosie's that Aussie guitarist Paul Lush appeared. He noticed I lacked a lead guitarist, and was a willing and excellent solution to that problem. With him, Chris on bass and Morgan on drums, and BJ Cole a happy collaborator, I started recording at Sean's fledgling studio, which started off in his girlfriend Maddy's run-down house in King's Cross (a whole studio running off one mains socket and a plugboard, as I remember) and then ended up in the house in Hackney where they moved to when they got hitched. Sean called the studio Famous Times.

A song that I had demoed earlier with BJ, *Everybody Is A Cowboy Now*, was fixed up with a new, improved tune, and it became the first track on the album, *Faithful*. The cover has me in front of the red flock wallpaper and curtain at the Golden Lion, gazing up pensively in my blue Wranglers. I hate it when people call me pensive, but they are right; I am. A lot of the songs were solo recordings, just me on my own playing acoustic guitar, with embellishments from the other musicians added afterwards. I was pretty happy with the result. Press coverage was thin, though, apart from a glowing review (kind of) in *Time Out* from Ross Fortune, which said lots of nice things but also said I looked "like a mutt terrier", which was news to me. I guess by inviting Mary Murphy's dog into the publicity picture I had invited the comparison.

Alan Tyler
'Faithful' Littlefield

With a goodly twang and lowly rumbledown swagger Tyler – the former Rockingbird (and latterday ubiquitous dude around town) – is one of the good terrier... I guess you pay the price. Dander, nary or nought.
 Hell. This is actually his first solo release. And anyone previously touched by his voice – such warmth and tenderness and sincerity and longing – will want to purchase a copy. Or two. (A spare for

The record eventually appeared in July 2002 on my own Littlefield (birthplace of Waylon) label, via the distributors, Proper. Richard Porter, a music biz ducker and diver who worked there and who knew Mike Stewart, set up a weirdly generous deal where Proper paid for the CD manufacturing, I owned the stock, and Proper had the sole right to distribute and sell it through shops. There was nothing for me to pay; nice one, Richard. Proper ousted Richard soon after that (one can only guess why), and the company sent me letters inviting me to pay for the manufacturing of the CDs, but I just ignored them. The 400 CDs that had already landed on my doorstep were more than enough for me, to sell at gigs and wherever else. I wanted for nothing more. Proper were welcome to sell the rest, or try to.

*

A strange character started appearing around my manor. A rotund figure, he always wore medieval clothes, with a green cape, a broad belt, tights, boots, and a trimmed full-set beard. He liked to enjoy a coffee sitting outside the Don Quixote cafe on Kingsway, watching the postmodern world go by. I thought perhaps he was one of the human statues who busked for tourists on the Covent Garden Piazza. Then one Sunday he turned up at the Folks, going by the name of Edward the Troubadour, and asked to play. Our resident rock'n'roll historian French Philippe spotted who he was – Teddy Paige from The Jesters, who had put out a single, *Cadillac Man,* on Sam Phillips' Sun Records label in 1966.

Teddy was from Memphis, Tennessee, but claimed to be from Sherwood Forest. It was a fiction he had maintained at school, where one of his pals was Jim Dickinson, the singer on *Cadillac Man*. Jim knew it wasn't true about Teddy being from ye olde England, but they were firm friends and fellow musicians. Jim went on to produce many great artists at his Ardent Studio in Memphis, including Alex Chilton, our hero from the Heavenly days, and played on many records that DJs would play at The Folks, like *Wild Horses* by the Stones.

Now Teddy was living as Edward in London WC2, in one of the local hostels for gentlemen of the road, with his three-wheeled Reliant Robin parked outside in Keeley Street. He busked here and there, and entertained us at the Folks many times, both at Rosie's and the Golden Lion. He would play his madrigals and English folk songs, and some rock'n'roll. One afternoon Chris and Big Steve put a band together for him and he headlined.

Edward wasn't going to stay around forever, alas. He had a few problems, and was prone to get into trouble. The National Film Theatre at the South Bank was screening a documentary about Jim Dickinson, and Jim and his sons from the North Mississippi Allstars were making personal appearances. French Philippe went down there, and Edward had the same plan. As Philippe got to the picture house he saw a kerfuffle outside; Edward had come with a dagger hanging from his belt, which had attracted the concerns of the London constabulary. Happily Jim and his boys came by and recognised their old buddy, rescuing him from his predicament. He ended up being introduced on stage with the rest of them at the movie screening.

Ivanhoe was a song inspired by our medieval friend. We were the English guys influenced by country roots and rock'n'roll from the American south, and he was from that musical heritage and longed to belong in Merrie England.

*"We're getting ready for the big revival
It'll all come clear
When the Mystery Train
Meets the old Beltane
For the big hit song next year"*

One warm, spring afternoon my girlfriend and I were sitting in Lincoln's Inn Fields with our daughter, down by Sir John Soane's Museum, when Edward came striding through the park. We shouted out to him and he stopped by, carefully raising each leg in turn to lift his rounded frame over the low wrought-iron fence to join us on the grass. We had just got back from our first visit to the new Tate Modern, we told him. Teddy growled a little; you could tell the mere mention of that gallery and all its contents disturbed him. "Why... that house of abominations!" was all he could say. After this righteous chastening for our corrupted tastes, he drew from his bag a small piece of art that he had produced. It was a finely-painted copy of the portrait of Richard III, the famous depiction of the last Plantagenet monarch, which he allowed us to hold and admire for a minute, before going on his way.

Since that day, whenever I pass by that museum of contemporary art standing by the River Thames, the quavering voice of Edward the Troubadour enters my head. *"That house of abominations!"* The voice grows louder each time.

*

Meanwhile, my job working for the government was going... OK. When my solo album came out, I had been in the Department for Education & Skills for a year. I had been moved up a grade to administrative officer, and was a permanent member of staff, still working for the ministers in Private Office. Our team managed recruitment, budgets and bills, and bought and paid for stuff: travel, including the Government Car Service (chauffeurs), catering, events, ministerial gifts (knick-knacks for visiting dignitaries) and ministers' wine (cheap plonk from Oddbins). The Secretary of State had a big office with about a dozen staff, and the other ministers occupied smaller offices on the same floor, each having five or six employees of their own. Private secretaries and assistant private secretaries kept their ministers' red boxes well stuffed with the daily influx of policy papers, and their diary managers and assistant DM's organised their every move. The five ministers under Secretary of State Estelle Morris were Stephen Timms MP, Margaret Hodge MP, Ivan Lewis MP, Baroness Catherine Ashton, and Lord Andrew Adonis. When Estelle Morris resigned in 2002, the ruddy-faced Charles Clarke MP took over.

Are you still with me, pop pickers? Are you bored?

More to the point, was *I* bored? Did I like the work? I didn't mind it. It was fairly low-level stuff, but there was plenty to do, and it generally needed doing. Most work is repetitive, and can be considered boring, looked at in a certain way. On the other hand, most work is absorbing enough and passes the time painlessly until it is time to do something perhaps more agreeable. "The busy bee has no time for sorrow". Work is work is work, and if you do it in an office, it's a warm place to sit in the wintertime. I had no objection. I am not proud.

I might object to pointless activity invented for its own sake. But even then, Winston Churchill laid bricks for his own amusement, and Horatio Nelson single-handedly dug out a pond in the grounds of his house in Norfolk, just to relieve his frustration at not being sent to battle. And the point is...? I think of a quip from *The Philosophy Of Andy Warhol (From A To B And Back Again),* where he says something like, "some people think it's sad that my friends sit around for hours putting makeup on their faces, but I think it's great, because it gives them all something to do".

One thing surprised me about civil service work, and the culture: I knew no civil servant could be entirely impartial, but I had thought they were professionally obliged to try to be, and to appear so. I had read Tony Benn's *Arguments For Socialism* in the 80s, which warned of a civil service "state within a state" that would obstruct the programme of a serious socialist government. But I found no performance of impartiality when I got there; we were all expected to get fully behind the government we served, and show our passion for the implementation of its policies. Much was made of "our mission" and "our values" and "going the extra mile". I just wondered... what will happen when the other lot gets in? Will we all be expected to perform with equal commitment for the Tories, and start going the extra mile with them in a different direction?

Spirit Of The West

SO I WAS a civil servant by day, and the Camden Cowboy by night (or at least on Sundays). After my usual lazy hiatus of a year or so after making an album, I prepared to go again and begin the next thing, but a major change had to be made, because Dave Morgan could not be with us. Out one night on his pushbike in Willesden, he had been run down by a vehicle that failed to stop. He was airlifted to the Royal London Hospital in Whitechapel with multiple injuries, and was in intensive care for a long time. Slowly he began to recover, but it was going to be a long road back.

Our search for another drummer led us to Phil Staines, who lived with his wife and two kids in a flat not far from the Camden Falcon, now long closed. Phil had been in psych-rockers Thee Hypnotics, drumming then under the surname of Smith. I dubbed the big man Phil Van Couver, after his Canadian hometown, and he didn't seem to mind. I also roped in Jim Morrison ("the one and only"). In 1993 we had invited accordion Slim to play on the *Rockingbirds 'R' Us* session, and Slim had brought his fiddle-playing bandmate Jim along, who proved himself a great improviser on both violin and mandolin. When Slim's Cyder Co came to play The Folks one Sunday about 10 years later, I wasted no time in nabbing Jim for our band. Paul Lush, myself, Fiddlin' Jim, Chris Clarke and Phil Van Couver made up the line-up for the new group: Alan Tyler & The Lost Sons Of Littlefield.

One place for us to play was the Tapestry Club, held on a Friday night once a month in the basement hall of St Aloysius Church in Euston. Built in the 1960s, the venue reminded me of my own church parish centre in Kenton where I had learned to do my drinking as a teenager, but this place was much bigger. It had wood-panelled walls, vinyl seating, a large parquet dance floor and a stage decorated with shiny *Phoenix Nights*-style streamers. The bar had a kitchen that would serve up sausages and other greasy delicacies that went round on a trolley each evening.

As with our Folks pubs, St Aloysius had its own regulars who welcomed us, or just tolerated us, as the mood took them. It was a favourite haunt of posties who came in before or after shifts at the Royal College Street Sorting Office. Though modern when it was built, nothing had been altered or updated since then, and that, of course, was how we liked it; tatty round the edges, but authentic.

The Tapestry Club was organised by our mate Barry Stillwell, who used to be one of the gang who ran the Sausage Machine at the White Horse, Hampstead. Barry hailed from Borehamwood, a north London satellite town not far from my old home in Harrow, and not unfamiliar to me, so I felt a local connection with him, a little like my Norfolk pals enjoyed among themselves.

Barry had an idea for putting on a festival. He had discovered a wild place – the Spirit Of The West theme park in Winnard's Perch, St Colomb Major, Cornwall. It was owned and run by a wild-moustached cowboy character who went by the name of Sheriff JB. JB professed to be a country & western fan, so Barry thought involving me with my country music credentials would help persuade the old-timer to let him host Tapestry Goes West there.

As theme parks go, Spirit Of The West was one of the most ramshackle you'll see, but it was remarkable for all that. It consisted of not one but two wild west settlements, Fort Smith and Silver City. It was like a western movie set, except that the saloon, the hotel, the courthouse and the jailhouse were substantial buildings, not just facades. Every year, JB and his family went to the States for six weeks – the only time they ever left their native Cornwall – and brought back more Americana and cowboy curiosities to add to their collection in the theme park's western museum. Added to that, Spirit Of The West had a stock car racing arena, a fishing lake, stables, and horses. Lots of horses.

JB ran the whole place with his wife, two daughters and just a few menfolk; one was betrothed to one of those daughters, and another, we were told, had escaped from Dartmoor Prison years back and was still a wanted man. Every afternoon the JB clan acted out a gunfight in Silver City for the park's paying customers, which on the day Barry and I went numbered about half a dozen. The rounds of ammunition in the outlaws' pistols may have been blanks, but they were as loud as live, and my ears were ringing long after Sheriff JB lay dead face down in the dust. Unmiraculously recovering, the local lawman rose again and ascended to the bench in the courthouse, where a park visitor was put on trial for his murder, found guilty, and led outside to be hanged. In the middle of the Silver City town square was a solidly-constructed gallows with a real noose, dangling and ready for a hanging, but it was not placed around the neck of the condemned customer – there was some consideration for health and safety, even in this wild, godforsaken place. At the last moment, the guilty party was pardoned and allowed to go free.

Barry's festival had two stages: Silver City was to have louder garage and rock'n'roll bands that were more typical of the Tapestry Club night (including Pink Grease, Part Chimp, The Beatings and the not-so-country Country Teasers), and Fort Smith would host less raucous country acts like The Arlenes, The Redlands Palomino Co. and Emily Barker. When we got there on the first day, Barry and JB were still banging nails into the unfinished Silver City stage. The flimsy piece of plastic sheeting over the top didn't look like it was going to do much good if it rained, which was threatening, but they got away with it.

I stayed in Fort Smith most of the time, organising the stage (which fortunately was already built) and the bands. On the first day there were only about as many people as a moderately busy Sunday at the Folks, with regulars like Lloyd, Tina, Plunket, Amy, Gerry, Nick, Hackett, Liz and Sergio all conspicuous in the photos. By my rough guesstimate I'd say about 200 people eventually arrived at the festival that first year, with maybe 500 the next, and a thousand at the third... which was when Barry and JB fell out over the money, ending our western adventure. JB was always very sweet and respectful to me, being the country music singing star that he thought I was, but I think with Barry it was a different story, and JB bared his teeth at him once or twice, and it got a little nasty. The next year, Tapestry Goes West went medieval, with archery, jousting and the Jim Jones Experience among the attractions at Margam Country Park in south Wales.

If you look online you will find a *Daily Mail* piece about JB's place; "Tumbleweeds Take Over Abandoned Wild West Theme Park". Photos taken in 2014 show it abandoned to the elements, with a litter of bottles and glasses in the barroom just as we had left it on our last day of festivities. A Facebook message I received from one of his daughters a few years later told me that proud JB, in exile from his western wonderland, was now a sickened, broken man.

But Tapestry Goes West was fabulous fun, such a hoot. Our Rolling Revue friend, Caroline Catz, now doing so well on stage and screen, shot footage on hand held film cameras and put together a documentary about it, the first of a number of fascinating movies she has made. As with Come Down & Meet The Folks, I'd say the festival was as successful as Barry wanted it to be, with neither high financial risks at the outset nor over-commercialisation at the end to come and spoil things. Hopefully he made a bit of dosh for himself, but as Barry said to me then, the main thing is to have a great time and be a hero for your mates.

We did get some complaints; there were few on-site facilities, no showers, and the catering was pretty woeful. JB's womenfolk who ran the canteen were more interested in looking after their horses than feeding us, and you were at their mercy if you wanted breakfast and had no car to take you to the nearest shop, which was miles away. The ladies were a little lacking in communication skills, the social graces that we metropolitan types are used to (politeness, in other words). They put up rude signs saying "NO WE ARE TOO BUSY TO STERILISE YOUR BABYS BOTTLE", and, on the gents toilet door, "PLEASE WASH YOUR HANDS AFTER GOING TO THE TOILET BEFORE TOUCHING OUR HORSES".

My band played each year, with our friend Mary Epworth joining us on vocals for the first of them. Although that first year was thinly attended, in subsequent years it livened up and we got good crowds and great receptions. Almost everyone wore western gear, of course. From the stage I introduced *Everybody Is A Cowboy Now,* observing, "Well, everybody really *is* a cowboy now". From over to my right there came one dissenting West Country voice, from a man standing on the porch of the general store in full Red Indian regalia and feather headdress.

Tapestry's last stand at Spirit Of The West brought our most successful Lost Sons performance. The night before, our exuberant Spanish friends Los Chicos had led half the festival-goers away from the stage in a mad, saxophone and drum led parade around the site. Tonight they were in the crowd for us, whooping it up with Caroline and other pals. JB was waiting in the wings, wanting to come on; I thought he just wanted to take a bow and accept a round of applause, which he deservedly got, but I had forgotten the small matter of JB's Rodeo Raffle. He and his company had been trying to sell tickets all weekend, and the first prize was impressive – a handsome leather saddle. Now was the time for the grand draw, much anticipated, so I thought, by no-one among our number, but it felt only right to indulge our generous host and play along with the proceedings. JB invited me to pick the first ticket out of his 10 gallon hat, the number was called out, and, unsurprisingly, nobody in the audience had it. The exercise was repeated, with the same result. And it was repeated, and repeated again. I doubted if many in our crowd had bought a ticket at all, but eventually, mercifully, a yee-haw went up, and a winner was found. JB departed at last, allowing us to go on with our set.

Somehow we managed to regain our musical momentum, and our gig came to a suitable climax and encore. Afterwards I was flushed and elated from our interrupted triumph, and JB found me and said he had a young lady who really wanted to meet me. Would I oblige? Expecting a CD signing, or perhaps something even nicer, I said I'd be delighted. The woman, who was standing by the saddle, was over the moon. "Oh Alan, that was *wonderful*," she enthused in a lilting Irish accent, "I have never, *ever* won a raffle before!"

*

When you tell someone you are from Harrow, they are apt to think you have somehow shared in the privileges enjoyed by those who have attended its famous school, the likes of Sir Winston Churchill, the poet Byron, posh pop singer James Blunt or gun-running Mark Thatcher, Margaret's son. In reality, the historic public school in the elevated village of Harrow on the Hill is remote from the rest of the London borough that shares its name.

Harrow is a densely-populated suburban sprawl, built around a few old settlements on what was once a rural scene. By the turn of the 21st century, the smart Metroland streets and houses, council estates, buildings and businesses were becoming shabby and uncared for. We Tylers were still stuck in the middle of it, and had done our bit in the spoiling of the area's pleasant garden suburb vibe by removing our old wrought iron gate and privet hedge, concreting over the grass and flower beds to make a place to park the car, and replacing the original front door and porch with ones of plastic, metal and glass.

Wanting to give a true account of the place, in the country music tradition of writing about the roots of one's raisin', I penned *Middle Saxon Town*.

> *"Up high upon a hill*
> *A famous school has done its trade*
> *From little boys great leaders there are made*
> *But we never wore that uniform*
> *School fees we never paid*
> *We only followed T Rex, Mud and Slade"*

I had been absorbing the changes that had taken place because I was now back living there. My relationship had broken up and I was out of the Covent Garden flat. After some sofa-surfing and a stay on Jon's boat, I resigned myself to living with my parents for a time, where my daughter could come and stay with us at weekends.

Middle Saxon Town appeared in 2006 on *Alan Tyler & The Lost Sons Of Littlefield,* our first release on Hanky Panky Records, a label based in Spain. Iñaki Orbezua had emailed me from Bilbao, saying he ran a small label, and did I have anything that they could consider for release? They might have been looking for some old Rockingbirds relics, but they didn't sound disappointed when I replied I had two new albums ready for release – the Lost Sons album, and an acoustic collection, *So Far*.

Things went nicely from there. Hitherto, Hanky Panky had been a collectors' label, re-releasing old obscurities and forgotten classics. They had just reissued solo albums made by members of 60s hitmakers The Honeybus: Pete Dello's *Into Your Ears* and Colin Hare's *March Hare*. Iñaki sent me copies, and I fell in love with them both. Dello's album is a minor masterpiece of English pop, the missing link between Ray Davies and Brian Wilson, and *March Hare* is also a delight. I was happy and flattered to find myself in such company.

Alan Tyler & The Lost Sons Of Littlefield was recorded in Chris Clarke's studio, which was then in the basement of the Stroud Green flat he rented from Neil Conti, the drummer in Prefab Sprout. Chris was a great supporter and friend, and put a lot of energy into making things happen for us. As well as producing our records, he hunted down a publishing deal for me; it was only a small advance, a few thousand pounds, with Bucks Music, but Bucks are respected independent music publishers, and I have done alright with them. I even recouped my advance, and had my contract renewed (a first for me), thanks mainly to a Lost Sons song lucratively placed in a German documentary film about ageing

Hell's Angels. Bucks and I are still waiting, of course, for my elusive hit, but this ultimate success needs to be put off a little longer now, lest it undermines the premise of this book.

When the record came out, a colleague at work I had never properly spoken to before came over and alerted me to the five-star review we had received in *Record Collector* magazine. This was Xerxes, who had been in punk maverick Johnny Moped's band. Civil servant John Skinner (his real name) had somehow exempted himself from open-plan office life, enjoying the privilege of a side-room of his own. The room was hardly salubrious, being full of old cabinets and computer junk, but it allowed him to read his newspapers and magazines in peace, when not standing outside Caxton House, smoking.

It was another luminous review from Terry Staunton, which flatteringly compared *Middle Saxon Town* to work by fellow north London hillbillies The Kinks. There were other good reviews, but despite these, some enthusiastic endorsements and a few plays on the radio, the album went the way of all the others before and since, which is to say, not very far.

I have often wondered, if my music can be genuinely admired and enjoyed by persons X, Y, and Z, including among them journalists paid to be good judges and influencers in these matters, why is this appreciation not replicated through the population, which even at a very moderate ratio would translate into thousands of satisfied customers and a viable business model for my music? At times I have found it hard to resist the solipsistic hypothesis that apart from myself and the few active participants and admirers who make themselves known to me, there may not be anyone else out there at all.

I suppose that's what happens to the solipsist, the rest of the world just walks on by.

*

Sales figures would suggest differently, but I think my later recordings are better than my earlier ones; I think I have got better at it. I didn't like the first Lost Sons album that much. I did like our next release, *So Far,* a lot. Sean's idea was to record favourite songs from our live set acoustically, each one in a single take. I had made a big deal about recording the first Rockingbirds album "as live as possible", but now we had the competence to do it. Sean pressed the buttons and put down his parts afterwards, and Mary Epworth came in and added some vocals, but apart from that and one or two little fixes, it was live.

Hanky Panky Records got us out to Spain several times to do some nice short tours lasting a week at a time. We played a few times at Kafe Antzokia in Bilbao and the Wurlitzer Ballroom in Madrid, and at different venues in Leon, Valencia, San Sebastian, Santander, Burgos, Castellón, A Coruña and Barcelona. In Spain I was better known for my Lost Sons than for The Rockingbirds.

I still wasn't that well-known, though... I could have no illusions. We did a live TV stage show for RTVE, "the Spanish BBC", and there were no takers for the free studio tickets. To rustle up an audience, the production team did what they had perhaps done before; they drove out to the nearby college campus and somehow lured back a minivan full of students, who were carefully shepherded into a tight group between the stage and a TV camera and told to clap and cheer when we came on, to simulate a real audience.

We encountered a different kind of "fake audience" at one of our Norwegian festival appearances. We were always well paid and looked after at these festivals, but along with other UK country acts like our friends Los Pistoleros and the Redlands, we got used to thin crowds in front of the stage. Most of the Scandinavians who attended these weekends did not trouble themselves with the acts lower on the bill; they stayed away until the end of the night, when they would come out of the encampments in a home-brewed hooch-crazed mass to see the Norwegian country headliner or whoever the Texan hot-shot band was that year. But during one performance of ours (you usually did a couple at each festival), we were encouraged to see a crowd massing in the middle distance halfway through our set. Were we making a connection at last? No. The crowd that was gathering was not there for us, but to honour the winners of the weekend's line dancing competition.

The next day the local newspaper put things in perspective. A large colour photograph showed in close-up some rather full-figured ladies smiling broadly and strutting their synchronised stuff. In the distance, just in shot on the stage behind them, you could pick out Alan Tyler & The Lost Sons Of Littlefield.

Knockbacks like these would perhaps be of no significance if things didn't sometimes, tantalisingly, go my way. I did play to a very real, packed audience at the Hackney Empire in 2007, backed by the 40-piece BBC concert orchestra. I was honoured to participate in a special "Guilty Pleasures" night that also featured Suggs, Terry Hall, Cerys Matthews, The Magic Numbers, Les McKeown from The Bay City Rollers, Guy Garvey, Ed Harcourt, and The Whore Dogs backing band (with Hackett, John Niven, Martin Kelly and Nick Dewey). Also participating were Chas & Dave, the only act allowed to sing their own numbers, with whom I had the pleasure of sharing a dressing room. At their gracious request, I serenaded them backstage with a couple of Merle Haggard tunes. They were a pair of sweethearts, but I confess I can still never remember with confidence which one's Chas and which is Dave. How useless am I, sometimes?

On the night, compere Sean Rowley introduced me as "London's greatest country singer", and I heard a great roar go up as I launched into my song. When it was all over, at the aftershow party in the theatre bar, a few remaining orchestra players flattered me wildly by saying they thought my song had been the best one of the night. It was true I had given it my all, and Neil Diamond's *Forever In Blue Jeans* was a good fit for my voice, and it had seemed to go down tremendously well with the young, enthusiastic crowd. My approach had contrasted with the sullen delivery and moody mucking about in rehearsal of some of the other singers, which had failed to impress the orchestra guys. I had sung nicely, you see, like my mum had always told me to, and they liked that.

Hoping to read some more flattering things about me in the numerous press reviews the next day, I was to be disappointed. Nobody said anything bad about me, because hardly anyone said anything about me at all, being the not so well-known one on the bill. It was naive to expect anything else; a big break? My big break days were long in the past. I have gotten to repeat my Diamond cover a few times with The Whore Dogs since then, at Glastonbury and some other quite swanky affairs, and that is just fine by me.

The following year, the second Lost Sons Of Littlefield album, *Lonesome Cowboys,* again recorded at Chris's studio, came out. It was the better of the two, I thought; I liked it. It had more of the driving Waylon Jennings delivery that I was aiming for, and the songs were pretty good all the way through. I was pleased with the CD cover design too, a single red rose in one of my black roper boots, the top of which formed the shape of a heart. I thought the screenprint-style colouring of Sonia Kobal's design made the Andy Warhol movie reference in the title obvious enough, but no-one commented. I wasn't going to cry about it, though. Like it said in one of the songs, *Cowboys Don't Cry.*

Rockingbirds Reunited

IN 2008 HEAVENLY asked The Rockingbirds to join in their 21st birthday celebration, their coming of age, with a gig at the Queen Elizabeth Hall with Edwyn Collins. It was part of a programme of events at the South Bank with other well-known Heavenly acts. Of course, we said yes.

Everyone in the band had remained on good terms. That had never been much of a problem. Dave Morgan now lived in St Albans with his bass-playing girlfriend Ruth, making music with her and others in his Big Fish studio. Patrick was still living in Norwich at the same place, making things in his shed. Andy Hackett had moved his vintage guitar shop from the Angel pawnbrokers to Denmark Street; he still issued pawn tickets to hard-up musicians, at very reasonable rates, of course. Sean was always in demand with his studio and as a musician, Graham Coxon from Blur being one of the latest to discover his talents. Chris was doing music with me and was soon to relocate his studio to commercial premises in Ferme Park Road, London N8. Just as his song *Going To California* had eerily predicted, Big Steve Arlene and his family had gone to live in California (before moving to Nashville). Chris now did Come Down & Meet The Folks with me, held at the Apple Tree in Mount Pleasant, near the City. I was working in the Department for Work and Pensions in Caxton House, SW1. I had moved there on promotion as an Executive Officer in 2003, and so I had remained, at the lowest of managerial ranks, with the Tories now in government, and Secretary of State Ian Duncan Smith nodding "good morning" to one and all in the lifts. I had taken on a new, so-called "affordable" housing association flat in Stratford, East London, with a second bedroom where my home-educated daughter could come and stay – but with no pay rises, annual rent increases, and child support still to pay, I was in over my head.

The Heavenly gig went famously. We invited Dave Goulding down from Manchester to play one song, while Chris did the others. Drinking-wise, Goulding was now a reformed character, but the rest of us continued unrepentant. The event brought the band back together again; I thought a reunited Rockingbirds would be sure to bring more opportunities than The Lost Sons Of Littlefield were managing to attract, so I made my apologies to Phil Van Couver, Lushy and Fiddlin' Jim. Sony repackaged the first Rockingbirds album with B-sides and other tracks to make a deluxe double CD package, and *Uncut* interviewed us for a "where are they now?" type feature.

Gradually we assembled some new material, and started readying to record it. Chris's spacious new studio was the obvious place to do it, but there was a bit of argy-bargy about what "mate's rate" he should be paid. Opening a studio was a high-risk enterprise by this time; cheap home recording technology meant they could only charge the same as they did 20 years back – Bark cost £250 a day then, and still did now – and the trend was for studios to close, not open. Chris was brave to hazard the enterprise, and highly committed to making it work. We settled on something with him, and recording went ahead.

Chris had started playing bass with Danny George Wilson's new outfit, Danny & The Champions Of The World. Paul Lush had also been recruited. On Sunday 29th May, 2011, Chris and I were due to do the Folks together at the Apple Tree; it was a few days after my 50th birthday, and the Folks was providing a conveniently-timed party for me. Chris chose that morning to text me to say he was leaving The Rockingbirds to fully commit to Danny & The Champs. The news put a damper on the day, but we got on with it. It felt a little weird, but then things often do.

To be fair to Chris, he never had the best shakedown with The Rockingbirds. He had never been one of the original Camden gang, as it were; he was not on the first, "legendary" album, never went to Austin, and he had not been a recipient in our mini-jamboree of recording and publishing advances. He joined when we were at our apex, and, through no fault of his own, it had gone gradually downhill from that point onwards. Danny was offering Chris a chance at something he could make a full contribution to from the start. And Danny was really good. He was a day-job guy like me, I think, but he had greater professionalism and a more obvious talent set. Back in 1995 Danny and his brother Julian had offered to sideline their band Grand Drive to join The Rockingbirds and save us from our demise. It was a generous offer, and I declined not properly appreciating the gift that I was turning down.

Chris had been my greatest friend and supporter, but I had chipped away at his faith in me, one way and another. As well as getting me a publishing deal, he put a lot of work into organising gigs for the Lost Sons. He got a prison gig for us – inspired, of course, by Johnny Cash at Folsom Prison – but I cocked a snook at it for no good reason that I can recollect. He also worked out a fairly extensive UK tour to promote the *Lonesome Cowboys* album, but

I ended up cancelling most of it because of conflicts over my childcare commitments. As much as I loved my kid, I shouldn't have given in. Chris, a dad himself, didn't say as much, but he knew it, and so should have I.

*

The Hanky Panky guys offered to put out a 7" single on their Spring label. At first we went for the Quo-like *Fixing The Roof In Your Dream* as the A-side, then we changed our minds (rightly) and went for the strongest song, *Till Something Better Comes Along*. We gave Hanky Panky their new instructions but these were not adequately communicated to the Czech pressing plant, and the single came back with the wrong song. Then the re-press came back still with the song titles mis-labelled, which Hanky Panky had to doctor with stickers. It was a mess.

It was a good single, though, and it earned us a few plays on 6 Music's Marc Riley show. I was pleased to get an endorsement from the ex-Fall man, being an old fan. We took our new bass player, Mark Duncan, up to Salford to do a live session for Mr Riley. I wanted to do some new, untried material, just like The Fall always did for John Peel. I had taken a liking to an obscurity by Jerry Jeff Walker, *Don't It Make You Wanna Dance?*, and we decided to include it. Rehearsals had to go ahead without Sean, who, as was often the case, was too busy with paying work. He could make the session, though, and came armed with a saxophone. All would be fine, we were sure; Sean was the most professional of us all. We set up in Riley's studio and waited for our time to arrive. When it came to the Jerry Jeff song, and the cue came for Sean to launch into his unrehearsed sax solo, he came in on a wrong note and struggled to recover. It was an absolute howler, and that song – and live sax soloing – were from that day forth banished from the Rockingbirds repertoire; Sean can keep all that for Dexys, one of those other bands he plays in.

We did some more recording in other studios to finish the album, with Mark on bass. Mark had been in lots of bands, Jackie Leven's being a recent one, The Vibrators not so recent. Andy knew him from the guitar shop. Mark and his partner Mimi had a bungalow in Petersfield that was full of old guitars and instruments that he had collected, made or mended. I only had my left-handed Gibson J100 Xtra as a working guitar, but Mark took a shine to my old Gibson LG acoustic that I'd used in the old Rockingbirds days, and fixed it up for me. He and Mimi also made a big wooden cactus for our merchandise stall, which I later cheekily appropriated for my acoustic trio, the Alan Tyler Show.

With the album completed, we needed a label. I hoped to interest Tom Bridgewater's Loose, the main independent label releasing country and Americana music in the UK. Posh Tom (as people sometimes call him), with his genteel tones and ruling class connections, had always been charming and interested whenever I had met him; he had been a Rockingbirds fan. I sent him the recordings, met him at the Famous Cock Tavern next to Highbury & Islington station, and he agreed to release *The Return Of The Rockingbirds* on his label.

Hackett, however, was never quite content with this arrangement. Before the deal was done, he arranged to have a meeting of his own with Tom, at a pub somewhere, and wore a wire to secretly record their conversation, which was a little eyebrow-raising. One of the things Hack said he was concerned about was the use of © and ℗ ownership credits that go on the sleeve. I listened to his legalistic point without feeling qualified to make a judgement on it. Whatever Loose normally does with other acts, I thought, they could do with us. I didn't care, and neither did Loose, that much; in the end Andy got the credits the way he wanted.

After the release, out on tour playing guitar for Edwyn, Hackett visited every record shop in every town they played to check if our album was in stock, and blamed our new label when it was found not to be. I told Andy that most people now bought their records online, and that indie record shop owners just stocked what they pleased, but this failed to placate him. It was good that he cared, sure enough.

Being close friends, Hackett may have taken some advice from Grace Maxwell, who was a very astute manager for Edwyn and had always been very cute on all the legals. Grace and Edwyn now preferred to run things through their own label, AED, but what was good for them was not necessarily right for us. I had resisted the idea of a self-release; I had no money of my own to invest and suspected the administrative work would likely land with me, as VAT returns for The Rockingbirds once had in the 90s. My attitude was: let a willing and established label do the work, and give them a little encouragement by allowing them their crafty contractual ruses that might one day make them some money out of us. Let them have their pound of flesh, or at least a sniff of it, if any flesh there was to be had. Staying in the game, I thought, was the best we could do. The priority was to keep out of "no deal" jail, and pass "Go" even if there was no £200 to collect on the way through.

The truth is, as with my atypical experience with bookmakers, the music industry has paid out more to us than we have ever earned for them. The exact margins I may not be sure about, but, taking into account all the money invested in us by Sony alone, there can be little doubt. Looking at it this way, my musical enterprises have proven to be perversely profitable.

Tom called a meeting with Paul Buck from the Asgard agency to help us organise a tour. Our mate Paul had been our booking agent in the 90s, and notionally still was. He was now an established player, with The Vaccines being his biggest band. A shortlist of likely venues was drawn up, and there was a discussion about getting a press guy in. Tom said Loose usually did this in-house, but Hackett and Paul Buck urged us to get someone else, someone they knew, who would do it for less than a grand. Tom reluctantly agreed. Hackett said Tom's reluctance was because he wanted to charge the band for doing press himself, as a recoupable expense – one of those little ways labels have of making money. This may have been true, but Tom had done as we asked, so fair play. The outcome, however, was not what had been hoped for: the appointed press guy struggled to get any coverage. The "where are they now?" piece from a year or so before meant there was no further publicity credit in the bank from that important source. Apart from a few reviews, our press man drew a blank, and I heard that Tom rang him up and they had a row about it.

Things went completely down the pan with Hackett and Tom at Glastonbury 2014. A happy clan of Tom, Danny and various

Champs had gathered backstage on the Saturday night to congratulate new Loose signing Sturgill Simpson after his headline performance on the Acoustic Stage. Hackett then appeared amongst them, uninvited and presumably in full flight on his annual Glastonbury high. At first things were convivial, so I am told, but the atmosphere soured when Hack began to pepper Tom with difficult questions about his label's handling of our band. It was a regrettable encounter, and gossip soon came back from Glastonbury that did us no credit. From then on, all efforts on our behalf from Loose were effectively withdrawn; they did nothing further to promote us, we were never mentioned in their promo emails, and our tracks did not appear on their promotional CDs. They were done with us. Tom had had enough.

*

The tour proved harder to arrange than had been anticipated. Glasgow's Broadcast in Sauchiehall Street booked us (the Lost Sons had played there before) and a promoter in Stockton-on-Tees took a chance. Then there was somewhere in Manchester, somewhere in Bristol, and Le Pub in Newport, Wales, plus a London gig at the Boston Arms dancehall. Six days on the road. Unfortunately we would have to start the tour in Glasgow, and work our way back down – not ideal.

Dave and Mark were particularly unhappy about the poorly-planned itinerary; Dave still struggled with pain and discomfort since his accident, and Mark was never at his happiest far from his Hampshire home. On the first date of the run, our minivan left, early in the morning and surprisingly on time, from outside Hackett's place in Swiss Cottage, and we then picked Dave and Mark up in St Albans. I remember stealing a glance at the woeful looks on both of their faces as they gazed out of the window of the van, pulling out of St Albans as we hit the road for Glasgow. It was not heartening.

We were not all ageing men in the van. With Sean not always available for our gigs, including most of these, we had taken on young Patrick Ralla, who could cover the backing vocals and keyboards, and was a dab hand with a guitar as well. The talented Mr Ralla had come over to England from Germany with The Kinbeats, who put out a single on Edwyn and Grace's label. They had been due to release an eponymously-named album as well. AED had generously invested in a "Kinbeats" neon sign for their album cover and publicity, like one Edwyn had, but the band – in a spectacular act of self-sabotage worthy of The Rockingbirds – decided to change their name at the last moment. Their neon creation had no further use, and their album plans went west.

Hackett was the first Rockingbird to meet the Kinbeats, which were Patrick and his brother and cousin. To entertain our continental visitors, Hackett dusted off all his favourite German and Nazi jokes. The other two bandmates were appalled at this outpouring of anti-German hate, but Patrick thought it hilarious, and a great friendship was forged. Patrick did not drink when he first came over; he was living with a Christian sect in north-west London and had committed to a life of sobriety and celibacy for the maintenance of cheap bed and board. Before leaving Germany, he had avoided national service by pretending to be over-fascinated with guns at the assessment interview. Dismissed as psychologically unfit, Patrick was given his liberty. Now he was in The Rockingbirds, going by the nickname of Sticky (sticky bun – a cockney rhyming slang Mark invented for "Hun").

The gig at Glasgow Broadcast went acceptably. It was half-full, or half-empty, depending on your positivity, or lack of it. Afterwards, Sticky, Hackett and I had a look in the casino opposite our Premier Inn hotel. Hackett had a system: you bet on red or black at evens, and if it doesn't win, you double the stake and bet the same again, and if that doesn't win, you bet the same and double again, and so on, until you win... or get completely cleaned out. It is the oldest gambling system known to man. After three tries, Hackett was out of his own cash, and was compelled to risk our night's earnings and tour float, which he had in his pocket. Happily, at this fourth time of asking, his system came good, and all was put to rights. I had two more modest bets on numbers 1-12; the first bet I lost, the second I won, and then I quit. It was my only ever visit to a roulette table: I had always wanted to have a go, but roulette is never a good bet, as it is pure chance and the house always has the edge.

The next day the band gathered together and took a stroll down to Glasgow's Grand Ole Opry, taking a few photos before setting off on the shorter journey to Stockton. This gig had nearly been called off for lack of advance sales, which would have blasted a huge hole in our short schedule, so we had renegotiated with the promoter, who was now putting us on in the theatre's foyer bar. We arrived early and wandered the almost deserted high streets of post-industrial Teesside. There were lots of boarded-up shops, charity shops, pound shops; even a "pound pub" was spotted (or maybe that was in Newport). A few dozen people turned up for the gig. It could have been worse. The support band had been cancelled and Sticky Pat and I provided our own support with an acoustic set.

And so it went on. At the Manchester gig, in the upstairs room of some crumbling Victorian pub, we played to another "selective audience" (to employ that now overused *Spinal Tap* euphemism). That night, the Wise One got out the Mosrite Melobar for the first time, which he used on *Fixing The Roof In Your Dream*. The instrument was a cross between a standard guitar and a steel, with vinyl padding and a neck that stuck out at 45 degrees. The next day, in a bleak northern town on the edge of Saddleworth Moor, we managed to find a cafe that was open and would serve us hot food. Dave was bearing things stoically and mainly silently, but he made it known to me he wasn't happy, and touring like this was no joy.

It was hard going for me too, but it wasn't the travelling and discomfort that bothered me; I was well in body and didn't find it that demanding. It was the anxious hours before many of our gigs when we were left to wonder how many would turn up that weighed heavily on me. Even when fears were confounded and a good crowd showed, and we had a good night to remember in the end, the anguish beforehand was still to be endured, and I hated it. This was not a new problem, a new feeling; it had been so with the old Rockingbirds at times, and touring with the Lost Sons as well. On one tour, the Lost Sons went all the way up to Torridon near Ullapool in the Western Highlands of Scotland. The drive up through the mountains had been magnificent, but we got there to play only to the South African proprietor, a couple of Polish waitresses, and a handful of tourists. Many of my contemporaries in music are more willing to undertake such ventures, but they do not feel like sane endeavours to me, and my gut feeling will usually be: please. No more. Stop! This Rockingbirds run was only a week out of my life, but without reasonable expectations of audiences to play to, I would rather make music closer to home than have my ego pummelled by the world's indifference, town after town, day after day, on tour.

*

It is all in the mind, I suppose. I can even get anxious before a Sunday afternoon Come Down & Meet The Folks, though I ought to know by now that these invariably come good. I loved my Folks, but it's also true to say that financial necessity inspired the event's long running; for a long time (and especially at this time) I needed what remained of what I made on a Sunday to keep me in food and fags for the following week.

I had banked on upping my income by getting a promotion at work, but this hadn't happened, and was not going to. Competent in my job, I could always be relied on to do what was put in front of me, and make sensible judgments, but that was not how you got on. Promotion was mainly down to the stories you could tell in your application and then how you performed at the interview. Perhaps I lacked what Alan Bennett called "the necessary accomplishment of saying things one does not mean", which comes so naturally to the middle class. Whatever the reason, I was as woeful with a civil service promotion panel as I could be with a music press interviewer.

Business in the Department for Work and Pensions continued with the Tories much as it had under Labour. The big work in progress was Universal Credit, the unified benefit system to replace all the old ones. It was a sensible enough objective but a horrendously complicated undertaking, which mandarins had grappled with long before under the previous Labour administration. My new team was part of the Social Justice Directorate, which sounded slightly Labour-y, but then I suppose "social justice" can take many forms. The diversity agenda was gaining pace; I remember our first "Diversity Day" in our office, which included a picture quiz to educate us about the range of sexual orientations, disabilities and racial identities represented among well-known people.

Some civil servants do important and useful things like issuing passports, paying benefits, organising elections and even drafting legislation, but others just flounder about with little purpose, trying to find something new to do. Most managers I encountered were empire builders, always keen to take on new staff, which, if nothing else, would give them or their managers below them more management work to do. The annual reporting cycle, where each member of staff agreed objectives with their manager, was a time-consuming part of everybody's job. You were monitored on your performance throughout the year, and given a "box marking" at the end according to how you met your objectives and demonstrated the required "competences" demanded by your grade. In a very real sense, this reporting *was* your job, insofar as keeping your job and your prospects for advancement depended upon doing this well and talking about it in interviews. Reporting was the measure of your success. The map was the territory. Corporate creatures who focus their energies on convincing each other that they are "doing a fantastic job" rarely have cause to look beyond their remote realms of trusted data and expert advice.

It was always Year Zero in the civil service. "Housekeeping" demanded that almost all work from two or three years back was deleted from the shared drives. Change was fundamental; the oxygen on which the organisation thrived, always moving forward, like a great shark. "Business as usual" was anathema; to stay with the tried and trusted would mean our work would wither and die. Many directorates set up "Change" divisions, to move us from the old things to the new, but change could not be left only to them. Adapting to change or managing change were things we all had to demonstrate in our daily work; a good story about how you had changed something could get you promoted. Just doing a job without fuss was no good.

I had one manager, very kind and likeable in many ways, but in her work she was like a spider, always spinning. Your work would always come back with new things to think about, new people to consult. Spin, spin, spin. It was Parkinson's Law in action: the job took as long as the time in which you had to do it, so every process was prolonged for as long as deadlines would allow. It was called "adding value", and considering things from the point of view of diverse interest groups brought useful opportunities for us to show how we could respond and adapt, extracting the maximum industry we could from each piece of work. It was fertile soil in which so much present-day nonsense has taken root and flourished; parasitic upon people looking for things to occupy themselves with.

I was doing "comms" work for the team that managed the European Social Fund (ESF) in England, a huge European Union programme to help people into work. I also organised the meetings when the EU officials came over from Brussels to check that we were spending the money correctly. I understood my own job well enough but had limited grasp of what my colleagues were talking about when they spoke about theirs in the meetings. I am a single language monoglot and have no talent for grasping bureaucratese. When taking minutes (which I often did) I developed the dubious talent of writing down the words (invariably to my colleagues' satisfaction) without genuinely understanding what they were going on about. My team was based in Sheffield, so I usually did team meetings over the phone. My manager, a nice woman called Lynnette, advised me to make better use of my mute button, as the sound of my weary sighs in London were transmitted loud and clear to their Moorfoot meeting room via the conference phone.

The ability to master workplace and corporate jargon I came to admire in others as a kind of magic power. Hearing other people speaking quietly at a distance was another talent I lacked. The proceedings at team "catch-ups" held in open-plan offices I found mostly inaudible; colleagues whispered or mumbled their news rooted to their desks despite the weak urgings of team leaders to come in closer. So quiet were some that I wondered if they had benefited from some special training in it. To be truthful, I could not always make the excuse of not being able to hear. Some meetings took place at close quarters in small rooms, but I still found myself drifting off within minutes, despite my most earnest efforts to listen to, engage with and understand the verbal updates that so effortlessly emanated from my higher-ups.

Despite my obvious attention deficit, I did pick up on a few things that were going on. EU officials insisted all ESF programmes spend 51% of their funds on women, even the NACRO ones, which were to help prisoners, who are mostly men. When NACRO protested at this imbalance, the officials just stared back and refused to acknowledge any absurdity in their demand. Economic inactivity among females was the major problem to be tackled, that was how they saw it. All must be maximised for Mammon.

Statistics showed that thousands of "neets" – young people not in employment, education or training – had been helped by ESF projects into work, but I found it extraordinarily difficult to get the required case studies of individual successes from the programme providers, and this made me sceptical about the statistics. A visit I made to an ESF project that trained migrant workers to be cleaners did nothing for my faith in our work; the project struck me as gratuitously funded and exploitative, but my audit colleague told me it was quite within the regulations, which I am sure it was.

What did I know? Questioning the rationale of the ESF programme would do nothing for my advancement, and I needed to improve my situation. Help came to me from my friends Stephen Ferguson and Alison Vickers. Steve and Ali ran What's Cookin', a music event similar to the Folks that they had started in

Leytonstone back in 2004, and they were now taking their hand-painted banners and plastic floral adornments to a new venue, the Birkbeck Tavern in Leyton, where they were going to try their hand at running the pub, living in. I was invited to house-sit their place in East Ham in the meantime, and this enabled me to do a bunk on my unaffordable "affordable" housing association flat. Ali, incidentally, painted our Come Down & Meet The Folks backdrop, a fantasia of old Camden and western country landmarks which features a gospel oak, ghostly musician figures from the Harry Smith *Anthology Of American Folk Music*, a Joshua tree, and the Rocky Mountains in the distance. It's a wonderful piece of folk art and I love to show our artists and visitors around it, when they take an interest.

The Folks kept going at the Apple Tree longer than anywhere else. When Chris stopped doing it, for assistance I had guitarist Jimmy Pinch up from Totnes in Devon, followed by Big Steve, now back from the US, travelling down from Norwich, until the more sensibly local Patrick Ralla took over as my co-host. The move from the Fiddler's Elbow around 2004 had been at the behest of the Apple Tree landlords Scott and Raz. Situated in the old Clerkenwell haunt of Creation, Capersville and Megacycles, in a quiet side street near the huge Mount Pleasant Post Office sorting office, the pub offered a reasonably well-proportioned L-shaped interior for our gigs and a large pavement outside to accommodate the spillover of drinkers, smokers and noisy talkers. The licensees themselves, a garrulous double act, were also an attraction. Richard 'Raz' Cobbing from Gateshead had been a teenage trampolining prodigy, representing his country at world championships in the 80s, then switching to skiing before injury cut short his promising career. Aside from co-running the pub, he had a nice sideline job as a winter sports commentator on Eurosport. Lincolnshire lad Scott Baker was less clued-up about Americana and country rock than Raz, but came at it with equal enthusiasm, though he amusingly expressed a naive incredulity that he actually enjoyed "this country stoof". Scott knew more about hairdressing, which he had learned to do in the army. A bloody good hairdresser was Scottie. He left London a number of years ago, and my haircuts have been sadly wayward since his departure.

More than 15 years since the Folks had started – with the help of the characters just mentioned, along with Barry Everitt promoting at the Borderline, the 12 Bar Club in Denmark Street and a few other places – a scene for country and roots bands and artists from the UK and US was well established in London. When we began the Folks it had been hard to find the kind of acts that we were looking for, but now there were plenty. In addition to artists earlier mentioned, we had The Broken Family Band, Jason McNiff, Sid Griffin's Coal Porters, Southern Tenant Folk Union, The Barker Band, The Cedars, The Ugly Guys (former Kursaal Flyers), the Peter Bruntnell Band (and all the other combos guitar prodigy James Walbourne played in), The Storm Weather Shanty Choir from Norway, Wes McGhee, Sean Tyla, "Serious" Sam Barrett, Darren Hayman, The See See, Circulus, Hank Wangford, Amy Rigby, Wreckless Eric, Hungrytown, Dave Sutherland, Trent Miller and Norton Money. I have no doubt forgotten a significant few.

Some DJs, like French Philippe and Tony Two Eyes, were no longer about, but our old friend Ski (now adopting the "Squirrel Head" moniker) still came along, and we showcased veteran North American folk artists on his Hornbeam label: Tom Paley, Bonnie

Dobson, John Koerner and Jim Kweskin. Some of the names I've listed are fairly well known, most are not. Nobody went on to be a megastar after playing at the Folks, but that wasn't the point. Thousands of people came through our doors over the years, musicians and non-musicians, and enjoyed the gigs with a genuine community of music fans... that was the point.

After a year or so Scott and Raz left the Apple Tree and took over the nearby Betsey Trotwood on Farringdon Road. We kept the Folks at the Apple Tree, but the Betsey became the focal point for a lot of our friends and activities. The Betsey had previously offered perhaps the most ridiculously unviable venue in town; Plum Productions would put on three bands a night, with an oversized PA mixing desk perched on a bar sectioning off a large chunk of the pub's small basement, leaving room for only a tiny audience. In their enthusiasm, the new proprietors offered me the vacant role of in-house gig booker, but I was not enticed, not even with the promise of my own office. Set up the venue spaces properly and see who comes along, that was my advice. If you like the look of them, let them put something on themselves.

They got rid of the basement bar and installed a more sensible PA. Nothing much could be done with the three arched alcoves that people rarely sat in, but it was a more plausible gig space now, and the room became good for amplified bands and Northern Soul nights. The upstairs room above the main bar suited acoustic music and comedy. Hannah and Trevor Moss started the Lantern Society there, a better class of open mic that continues with others in charge. Foghorn Leghorn put on My Grass Is Blue, an unamplified bluegrass session. Henning Wehn previews his comedy sets there, but notorious comedian and conjurer Jerry Sadowitz prefers to troll audiences with new material in the basement.

Jon The Boatman and I did a couple of August 16th Elvis anniversary nights, using the whole pub. No silly Elvis impersonators for us; instead, we had a full-size cardboard cutout of the King in his gold lamé suit to greet everyone at the door. We screened concert movies upstairs, and held 'The Colonel's Tombola' in an alcove, stocking it with a job lot of memorabilia I bought off an old fan in Canning Town. Jon played Elvis records all night, each one better than the next, climaxing (as such events always must) with the cathartic *American Trilogy,* where everyone linked hands in a circle and sang along with the "glory, glory hallelujahs" (with a bit of cajoling from me.)

The Folks left the Apple Tree for a year, around 2010, when we were wrongly advised by the manager that it was going to close. We went to the Stag's Head in Dalston, but came back. The Stag was a chaotic old pub, almost like a squat. It was run by the irrepressibly generous Matty, who spent £200 in Sainsbury's every Sunday to lay on a free barbecue in the back. Consequently the pub attracted a large, young, hungry crowd, who were not always that interested in what we were doing.

That was the one time the Folks moved away from the course of the River Fleet, the once open and semi-navigable waterway that now runs underground from Hampstead through Camden and Clerkenwell. I remember it bubbled up once and flooded the basement in the Fiddler's Elbow. The sound of it gushing towards the Thames can be heard from a manhole outside the Coach & Horses pub in Ray Street, EC1, halfway between the Apple Tree and the Betsey. It inspired *Dark River*, one of my river songs, about the natural history of London and its environs, the more rural past that dwells in the urban present.

> *"Under brick, under steel, under tar, under stone*
> *Near forgotten and buried below*
> *From the high Hampstead reach*
> *To the Blackfriars breach*
> *In the darkness you rumble and flow"*

*

When Stephen and Ali had had enough running their pub and wanted to come home, it was time for me to move again. At the end of 2013, finding a place to rent was harder for me than ever. When I finally found something, my un-Cooperative Bank shafted me by declining my request for a bankers reference, losing me the flat and a £400 deposit.

I began to despair and considered the prospect of a return to Harrow once more, but a boat-dwelling Folks friend of mine, Vicki, threw me a lifeline – a link to a Gumtree ad for a houseboat to rent on Deptford Creek. Cheap accommodation? I was on the phone like a shot, and arranged to go down to meet the owners. I brought my now teenage daughter along with me; a berth was going to be needed for her as well, and Christina was a bright little charmer who I thought might help our cause. The meeting went amiably, we said we'd love to take it, but next day I got a call saying "Sorry", it had gone to a more experienced boater. I said "OK", but if there was any problem, let me know, and we would absolutely take it. The next day I got a call saying the experienced boater was dicking them about, so we were in.

Deptford Creek is where the River Ravensbourne comes out to meet the Thames on the south side. It is on tidal waters (unlike the canals and waterways where most boat dwellers live) and the boat was not a barge or a narrowboat but an old fibreglass cruiser. It was on a fixed mooring, going nowhere, complicatedly tied up to adjacent boats, which were among a dozen in number on that part of the creek. A boat on our port side was owned by an ex-merchant seaman who I rarely saw. The one time I spoke to him he went on about rats: there were a lot of them, hundreds, between the mooring and the nearby Birds Nest pub, and they could eat through the side of your boat, even through concrete, and sink it, so he said. In the boat on our other side lived Eddie Real, the former percussionist of the Alabama 3, who was much more neighbourly than the other fella. I heard the trip-trap of Eddie's Crocs on my roof at all hours; he had to walk over my boat to get to the gangplank on his way to or from wherever he was going (usually the Birds Nest). I didn't mind; I liked it all.

In the adjacent yard, part of the former Evelyn Wharf, there was a communal house where all the mail got delivered and several caravans, huts and other contrivances that people made homes in. These were on land nestling under the concrete arches of the DLR railway, which probably accounted for the survival of this off-the-grid enclave. Other moorings along the creek had been lost to property developments that had cut off their access, but the DLR flyover made it difficult to build here, though I fear developers will eventually work out a way.

The Birds Nest on the corner of Creekside had been a mainstay of the Deptford pub gig scene since the 70s – local heroes Dire Straits had played there, once upon a time. It now had a shady, shabby and forbidding appearance, the sort of place most people would think twice about entering. Even I, walking past for the first time with Christina on the day we viewed the boat, considered it a little doubtfully. Hackett, on the other hand, showed no such uncertainty when I first introduced him to the place. He immediately took to its extremes; a pub at the edge of the world.

Along with local boaters and other creeksiders, the Birds Nest attracted a few students from Goldsmiths up the road, random gig-goers and numerous south London squatter types and itinerants, the delightful and the dubious. The hard-core regulars huddled inside in the winter months, and when it got warmer larger groups gathered around the wooden tables out front for beers, smokes and whatever else. Inside and outside, posters for gigs and local events were stuck up on windows and walls, and the men's toilet walls were so thoroughly graffitied that it had become a three-dimensional work of abstract expressionism. There was a pool room at the back that doubled as a gallery for local artists of variable talent (the old buildings along Creekside were full of artists' studios). The stage and gig space was small, stuck awkwardly between the pool room and the long, central horseshoe-shaped bar, which was the pub's great asset. The bar brought customers into close proximity and encouraged interaction. Sadly, during the Covid restrictions a few years later, these virtues came to be considered a problem and the decision was made to take the bar out completely and replace it with one along the side, in order to enable the legally required "social distancing". The removal of the old bar left it a better functioning gig space, perhaps, but it felt like a lot of the heart and soul of the pub went with it. There is now, I am advised, talk of it being put back.

The other thing about the Birds Nest (well, one other thing) was the hostel above. Dormitory accommodation of the most insalubrious kind was offered at rock-bottom rates, and some of the pub's more down at heel customers were also its residents. The rodents who were sometimes to be seen in the bar also, no doubt, found their way upstairs. Sometimes unsuspecting tourists would book themselves in, to their regret. Eddie and our mutual mate Dave the Hat would amuse themselves from time to time by reading aloud the hostel's hilariously bad reviews on Tripadvisor.

The far more desirable comforts and facilities we enjoyed on the boat included an electricity hook-up and some solar panels that I think ran the shower pump. Everything was a little complicated, Heath Robinson-like. Water came from a shared plastic mains pipe which the old tar, Eddie and I used to replenish our water tanks. I had to keep an eye on that; if my tank ran low, the tap water came out brown. We had a macerating toilet which pumped our shredded sewage into the creek. It was a dirty secret between our boat and Eddie's, but the owners said it was legal on the tidal Thames. The gas cooker ran off Calor gas and I had to wheel the heavy bottles on a trolley to Deptford High Street to get refills. In the winter the stove worked nicely; I bought bags of coal from Wickes on Blackheath Hill and was always on the scavenge for wood and kindling to get my fires going. Most things didn't work that well, but the delight was that they worked at all. I didn't have to be too clever on the practicals and maintenance because the owners lived on a neighbouring boat and wanted to take care of all that. They just wanted me to keep everything clean, which in the end they gave me shit about not doing, but never mind.

The boat had a low ceiling which meant inside I had to stoop a little bit more than I usually do, but at the front you could raise the roof and stand up straight and let the air and the sunshine and the creek-stink in. One day I opened it up and a melody blew in across the bows, and I set some words to it and called it *Down On Deptford Creek*.

> *The water's rising with the tide*
> *That comes in twice a day,*
> *The city streets are always near*
> *But now we drift away.*
>
> *From muddy beds we're lifted up*
> *In boats that crack and creak,*
> *It's time to strain the ropes again*
> *Down on Deptford Creek.*
>
> *And though the wind is blowing low,*
> *And though my light is weak,*
> *I'll see a moving picture show*
> *Down on Deptford Creek.*
>
> *And when the tide begins to turn*
> *And goes back to the sea,*
> *A mossy wall shows velvet green*
> *That used to be the quay*
>
> *Where bigger boats had once come to,*
> *When Ha'penny Bridge was raised,*
> *Unloading cargo from afar*
> *Back in the older days.*
>
> *Below the rumbling dockland train,*
> *Down in the waters bleak,*
> *I see the ages ebb and flow*
> *Down on Deptford Creek.*

And when the sea has left the scene
It leaves a shallow flow,
Where duck and wader, gull and grebe
And herons come and go.

To pick among the rank remains
For filthy foraged fare,
In tangled twine a Christmas tree
A broken office chair.

Up on a rung my fisher-king,
Above the sea-birds' shriek,
Surveys the silver in the stream
That swims in Deptford Creek.

A flash of blue, a dip, a dive,
A tiddler's in its beak.
I hope that I'll see you again
Down on Deptford Creek.

Happily established on the boat, another stroke of good fortune was coming my way. The Tories wanted government departments to shed staff, thousands of them, under their austerity programme. In the Department for Work & Pensions voluntary redundancies were being offered under the terms of the Civil Service Compensation Scheme. In other words, they were going to pay people to leave, with "compensation" calculated according to what you had earned and how long you had been there. I applied, as many other colleagues did, not knowing if I would be selected. Not many of us were, but, by chance or some unseen hand, I was. I was leaving, I was out of there, taking a lump sum and a small monthly pension as well. Free again.

*

The next year, 2015, was my busiest-ever year, music-making wise. I had money to record whatever I liked, and had three albums on the go. The first two were made at Bark Studio. *The Alan Tyler Show* was a £5 budget sampler CD for my new light-travelling acoustic trio of me, Jim Morrison and Patrick Ralla. The CD featured acoustic versions of my river songs and cover versions like *Tecumseh Valley* and Buddy Holly's *True Love Ways*. The same trio also recorded *William Blake's Songs of Innocence*, faithful renderings of all 18 of the visionary artist's poems, published for free on YouTube with each song visually accompanied by its respective print. Emma Tricca, Siobhan Parr and Bryony Afferson came in to the studio to add a variety of voices. They all sang beautifully, in their different ways. Briony singing the *Laughing Song* is my most listened-to thing on YouTube. We performed *Songs Of Innocence* once, live at the Deptford Cinema, a volunteer-run flea pit which later closed because of the Covid lockdowns.

The third album I was working on was the next Rockingbirds effort, but this proved to be the difficult one. We worked out the guitar parts for the new songs in Hackett's shop, Andy, me, Mark and Sticky, having fun and retiring afterwards for beers in the beloved and much missed 12 Bar Club, a couple of doors down. We had a good feeling about what was coming together, but sadly this feeling wasn't shared by Dave Morgan, who felt out of the loop.

When full band rehearsals commenced at Alaska Studios in Waterloo, the atmosphere failed to improve. Dave enthused about his involvement with Mark Perry's ATV, but showed no such enthusiasm for our stuff. He scorned our only half-serious jokes about going "pub rock"; perhaps he had had too much experience of real pub rock in the small pond of St Albans to want to go into that territory with us. Dave also had an aversion to charlie. At one rehearsal the white powder appeared and was partaken of, except by Dave, whose disapproval I failed to register. Without telling us, he went on a "work to rule" in protest, playing his drums mechanically and without embellishment. I thought his new economical approach sounded great, and said so, and this confirmed for him that my judgement was shot, straight through the nose.

Recording started at Famous Times. Sean had a plan about recording the whole band live with the drums playing to click tracks, but Dave wasn't agreeable; he wanted to get his parts down as briskly as he could and go. He talked about there being "bad vibes" in the studio (which could not then be disputed). He did a good job, but it had been done his way, not as we had planned.

For a long time afterwards, I regretted not calling a complete halt to the recordings after the trouble on day one; I was upset about the disharmony with my dearest friend and had lost heart. It didn't feel worth doing if we were not all committed, and especially if Dave was unhappy. We soldiered on, with generous production guidance in the studio from our friend and former Oasis guitarist Gem Archer, but when it was finished I did nothing to press forward for its release, and consequently nothing happened for a few years.

In the end the fourth Rockingbirds album came out in 2019 as *More Rockingbirds* on the Hanky Panky label, with most of the drums re-recorded by our new man Stuffy Gilchrist. A few gigs came in and I had to ring Dave up to say why he wasn't doing them with us; he was out of the band. We had a disagreement; he had his things to say, and I had mine. We were not meeting in between. It was no fun. *More Rockingbirds* is a good album, and tracks like *In The Back Of My Mind, Deptford Creek* and *When The Winter Comes* were well-received by a few enthusiastic fans. I was happy to get out and play when the opportunities arose, and I still am, but I had other things that I wanted to do.

Yesterday's Chips

WHAT WAS THE point of it all, this singer-songwriting? This pop music making? What was I trying to do? And where did we go from here? Was it down to the lake?

If asked what it was all about in my Rockingbirds days, I would have said something perhaps slightly pretentious about putting something beautiful into the world, something the world had not seen before. Not an ignoble aim (in amongst all the prosaic, selfish motivations, obviously), but certainly not radical.

Before that, in the 80s when I was in Take It, we took pride in our left-wing radicalism, and plotted to infiltrate the pop charts and the Labour Party. My Labour Party membership ended in 1985 after the miners' strike. The miners had to win at all costs this time, party activists agreed, or the power of the working class to affect socialist change would be destroyed. But when the miners lost, those dire predictions were forgotten and some comrades even hailed the strike as a moral victory to steel us for the struggles ahead. This shape-shifting duplicity was too much for me, and I left my Crouch End comrades to continue their struggle without me.

As the years went by, with the coal mines closed and our industrial base decimated, Thatcher's defeat of the working class labour movement was confirmed, but the middle class left went marching on and on. Our band fizzled out, but left-wing entryism into pop music continued and ended in complete victory. You do not see pop stars and TV celebrities at the Tory Party conference like you once did – they would no longer be seen dead there. Liberal-left progressive assumptions prevailed, not only in entertainment but in all other industries and worthy professions, even among supposed Conservatives. The long march was over. The only problem was that a lot of ordinary voters did not share in this new enlightenment, voting for successive Tory governments in futile defiance of the right-thinking folk who had taken control of most other things.

*

"No one is bored; everything is boring."

In a talk given in Zagreb, recorded and published on YouTube in 2014 as *The Slow Cancellation Of The Future,* music critic and Marxist cultural theorist Mark Fisher (blogging alias k-punk) riffed on the decline of popular music, culture and society, much of it the result of over-reaching technology working in the service of capital. In the post-modern present, he argued, pop music fails to sound new anymore. New genres do not spring up as they once had; the "sense of culture belonging to a specific moment" has disappeared, and even 'the future' has become a thing of the past, like Concorde and our old Kraftwerk records. What we have now is "20th century culture distributed by high-speed internet". Tech allows us to re-create the sounds of previous eras, and so we do. Retro is universalised, and therefore nothing is truly retro at all. We are stuck on our smartphones in an endless present, inundated by media micro-stimuli; hundreds of daily alerts and commands that distract, direct and demoralise us.

Fisher's *cri de coeur* might be dismissed as intellectualised grumpy-old-manism. It can hardly be denied that the former accelerationist philosopher and jungle fan was deeply disillusioned with the state of things that had come to pass, and was now having a rant about the shittification of everything. But though he was wary of nostalgia, Fisher thought credulousness about the present the greater danger. We should not underestimate our dissatisfaction with our situation, he concluded, even if politicised melancholia, a refusal to adjust, is the only available protest.

There was an air of pre-culture war inertia about the talk, even though, politically, things were by that time starting to heat up, with Fisher one of the earliest protagonists. In his 2016 essay *Exiting The Vampire Castle* he defended Russell Brand from lefty finger-waggers on Twitter, flatly rejected identity politics, and lamented the embourgeoisement of the left and popular culture. It was his last stand against the vices his comrades were succumbing to, because in 2017 he took his own life.

I parted company with Fisher on his revolutionary aspiration to overthrow class society, considering it neither doable nor desirable, but I still agreed that class shapes our experience and motivations, and without a keen sense of that, we are lost trying to understand ourselves and others, and how the political world goes round.

The cultural disappearance of the working class was something that had long been bothering me. So much that was great about 20th century popular entertainment and music was the self-taught talent of artists of humble origins who flourished and made their mark. This was true of dirt-poor blues musicians and country singers in the USA, and also of nationally-beloved British TV and radio entertainers who had learnt their trade treading the boards in music halls and variety clubs. All of The Rockingbirds were self-taught (as was the norm among our contemporaries) but the age of the autodidact was now in decline. There is no money to be made from letting people learn and do things for themselves, so when Tony Blair came to power, promising "education, education, education", his administration plugged that gap in the market, professionalising popular music production with the creation of pop schools where young adults paid to be taught what their more successful predecessors had learned for free. Since then, working class representation in the arts has faded, and what is produced is more safe, more middle-class, more predictable, and more shite. But that is progress; capitalism is all about parting people from their own knowledge and abilities so that they can be turned into consumers of whatever its growth industries want to sell back to them, and education is one such industry.

Which is not to say that no-one who emerges in this new era is ever any good, that would be silly – and I have been silly that way, I do admit. I tend not to pay much attention to new stuff, and missed out on Amy Winehouse while she was alive, learning to love her only after she was gone. But the cultural and business environment for new music and musicians has deteriorated, I think most would agree, and it is not just because musicians are expected to share their recorded product for free (though all these things are connected). Nothing is epoch-making. There are (to use Fisher's phrases again) only subtle modulations, no great sensational shifts. It is true even of rap, which, as music genres go, may be more vital and autonomous than most.

So what was left for me to do? Marx said the point was not to interpret the world, but to change it. The problem, as I was coming to see it, was that we were now so intent on changing the world that we were failing to interpret it, failing to see it. Blinkered by unacknowledged class-based prejudices and politicised thinking, we were getting a lot of things horribly wrong. My emerging "our side are not always the good guys" point of view was unlikely to make me popular, to be sure, but I found myself compelled to make my melancholy stand, to testify, to have a tilt.

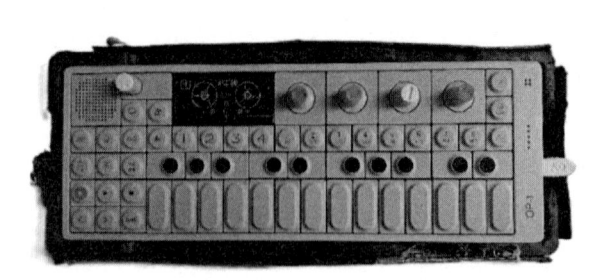

*

I did not mention it before, but back in my swingy, jazzy 80s days I had a sideline dalliance with electronica. With some of the money I had made from tap dancing I bought two silver boxes of microchip music-making technology, which at that time were sold as the Roland Bassline and Drumatix. With these I composed and synchronised bass and drum patterns like the ones on my D Train and Sharon Redd records. Playing them back through the stereo, I impressed a few house guests, including our dope dealer friends Kenny and Tao, who on their last visit to our place went downstairs to let one of their associates in to burgle my shiny music boxes, and my electro-dance experiment came to a sudden end.

The Bassline became better known as the TB-303, a definitive acid house sound-maker. Had I held on to my music tech a little longer, I might have donned a smiley face T-shirt, made a pile of money doing dance music, and the rest would not have been history. Kenny and Tao had averted that frightful outcome, but by 2016 I had a hankering to boldly go back to where I had previously gone before, and asked people on Twitter what programmable synth set-ups were recommended. Friendly fellow music maker Darren Hayman replied, saying the Teenage Engineering OP-1 was supposed to be good, so I looked it up, liked what I saw, and bought one in the Conran Shop for £600.

Now no longer in production, the OP-1 is about the size of two large smartphones laid end to end, with a keyboard, a little screen and a row of sturdy knobs. It has scores of modifiable synth and drum sound presets which you can play, sample, program and record onto the machine's four tracks of digital "tape", which roll for six minutes. After a week of bafflement I got the better of the thing and commenced endless hours of electronic music-making. My efforts may have been unsophisticated and primitive, but what did I (or anybody else) care? It sounded great to me. Didn't Hawkwind get the seminal *Silver Machine* Moog sound almost straight out of the box? Weren't the Human League the first to use programmed Linn drums in pop? The fresh sounds and approaches that come with new instruments and technologies are inspiring, and the OP-1 offered what felt like an entirely new dimension of abundant options that allowed me to forge ahead to make a new record on my own.

Instant gratification and complete control are enjoyable aspects of the process. When you programme music yourself, your drummer is working to your own rule, and no other musician is varying things or throwing in little extras that you don't want, just because they are getting bored. It brings you closer to the mantric essence of pop, which is repetition. Repetition. Repetition.

The OP-1 allowed you to overdub infinitely onto the four tracks, so the risk of sonic over-indulgence was obvious. I set down some rules of engagement early on. My idea was to compose four basic drum and synth tracks for each song, and then take it into Sean's to set them with acoustic guitars and voices. Electric and bass guitars were not going to be allowed, a rule I stuck with. Some songs stood up without a bass line, with the fat strings of the acoustics and the thump of the bass drum doing the work at the bottom end.

"Post-truth melancholia with electro hooks and country harmonies" was what I called it, though looking back I see this not-so-memorable catchphrase was rinsed from the album's press release. It is best to leave these things to the professionals, of course. My journalist amigo Andy Fyfe did that for me, writing a bio which stitched some of my own garbled words together to explain the concept of *El Tapado*.

> *"What's El Tapado? Well, I was thinking about Dark Horse as a title, because I've been called a dark horse in the past and I hate it. HATE. IT. It suggests something suspicious and underhand. So I googled it in Spanish and 'tapado' came up. Turns out it means 'covered' and I thought, I can go with that. But in Mexican street slang it means dumb fuck, dumb ass, ignorant bastard, and I can really go with that."*

A little before *El Tapado's* release, I was chatting to Fiddlin' Jim after a gig in the Birds Nest. I expanded on my concept of Tapado as a bold but hapless truth-teller who calls out the lies of the world but may be equally deluded, or is denounced for so being. We hit upon the idea of Tapado the pro-wrestling persona, the kayfabe superhero, a 21st century saintly fool. I shared the vision of my quixotic caped crusader on Twitter, and a friend provided a link to online cape-buying options. I bought a silver hooded one, cut out the letters of EL TAPADO from my gingham vinyl tablecloth, blacked them with marker pen, and got Christina to stitch them on the back with her sewing machine (the publicity photo that resulted is actually of my daughter, caped and hooded, with her back to the camera and face concealed). At the album launch at the Heavenly Social, I made my silver-caped entry through the audience, clapping my hands above my head to the hi-energy beat of my gender role-questioning anthem *To Be One Of The Boys*. It was a song I had tried to get my publishers to enter for Eurovision, without success.

> *"It's good to be one of the boys.*
> *Good to be one of the boys.*
> *You'll always be one of the boys.*
> *Always be one of the boys."*

On the stage with Sean, Patrick, and the OP-1 was Angie Gannon from The Magic Numbers – not one of the boys, obviously, but a contributor of vocals to the album. She sang on a retake of my old song *Lucky Lonesome*, a cover of Sissy Spacek's *Hangin' Up My Heart,* and also on *Going Back To Mexico,* which made topical allusion to Trump's wall but was more about a poverty-trapped Londoner returning to her home town, thinking about the sunnier adventures of her youth. Iñaki at Hanky Panky helped me translate some of the words into Spanish:

> *"It's not far at all*
> *Up and over the wall*
> *Adiós a los bastardos*
> *Navega sobre el mar*
> *Donde querias estar*
> *Saborealo mi amigo"*

My Heart Was Always Wrong was my tale of love as irresistible and recurring folly. The Trump era post-truth folly I took on more directly in *Shattered* and *I Don't Dream*.

> *"We got a phoney*
> *We get baloney*
> *Boney Maroney*
> *Was more my scene"*

Like everyone around me, I was horrified by Trump's election. How could a politician so estranged from the truth now lead the western world? On TV, comedian Stewart Lee walked dazed and confused through London streets in a send-up of our collective Trump election shock, exactly as I had done on the morning of Trump's victory. That month I had moved into a properly affordable one-bedroom garden flat; a permanent and very acceptable place of my own. My serial-renting woes were at an end, but what good was such fair fortune now that the age of existential dread had dawned? Stunned by the ghastly news from the United States the night before, I walked out through my peppermint-painted front door on the morning of Wednesday 9 November, 2016, headed down the hill to New Cross Gate, and shambled onwards, with a cloud of doomy, desolate thoughts hovering just above my head.

Continuing Thames-wards I came to Surrey Quays; perhaps an unconscious want for retail therapy was drawing me. Around the corner was my favourite men's outfitters, Jays Stores, purveyors of reasonably-priced workwear, Wrangler trousers, button-down gingham shirts, monkey boots and quality Harrington jackets. As the shop came in sight, I saw the colourful hand-painted signage I was looking for, with its jeans-wearing gentleman as its centrepiece, but when I arrived my end-of-the-world forebodings were confirmed; Jays Stores had closed down.

*

By the time *El Tapado* came out, there was something even more bewildering than the election of the pig in the White House to ramp up my growing disbelief and despair at the dystopian present. And no, I am not talking about bloody Brexit, I am talking about the great idiocy of the 21st century, gender identity.

Imagine a sci-fi story where a man awakens from a long coma to find people no longer recognise the real differences between men and women, and it has been deemed a crime to deny a man is a woman if he declares himself to be one. Not long ago such a scenario was too far-fetched for any fiction writer to have envisioned, or for any social soothsayer to have wished for or warned against, and yet, suddenly and with no noticeable warning... here we were!

Gender ideology (by which I mean everything we are expected to think about "gender" today that nobody thought until a few years ago) had been quietly accepted, affirmed and put into policy by the judiciary, the police, the military, academia, the media, nearly all people in government and the civil service and most major corporations, which just shows how gullible, compliant and thoughtless such leaders and institutions can be. Outside the Vampire's Castle, Mark Fisher had protested, there are "no identities, only desires, interests and identifications". Sadly, he had been pushing against the techno-capitalist tide, and it was his colleagues on the left who championed the new gender politics with the greatest zeal, providing as it did new opportunities for employment and profit for people of their own class. Dim-witted middle class generalists could now teach the 57 varieties of gender in schools and offices, providing a steady stream of "educated" young consumers for the "trans health" industry; fully qualified quacks selling thousands into lifetimes of gender-affirming medication in pursuit of their "authentic selves".

When it comes to make-work capitalist rackets – costly and harmful solutions to newly identified or invented problems –

"gender" is one of a number, with gain-of-function viral-research probably the most catastrophic. You do not need a bookmaker's nose for probability to realise the lab leak hypothesis for the origin of Covid-19 is an odds-on racing certainty. Any damn fool can tell you that manufacturing viruses to be more contagious and deadly than naturally occurring ones is a terribly dangerous thing to do, and that the emergence of a novel SARS-like coronavirus in the main place in the world where scientists were making them, Wuhan, points firmly and obviously to a laboratory genesis. Unfortunately, there are many people of great intelligence and influence who prefer to believe the sophistries of those involved in such research, the scientists and their funders who profit from it, who have fiercely denied the Covid-19 outbreak could have had anything to do with them, who have stood in the way of any full and open investigation, and who have done everything in their power to censor and suppress any words which might impute against them, which they proclaim to be hate-crimes against science itself.

In a godless age, doctors and scientists are our most revered citizens; it is unthinkable that those we trusted to guide us through the pandemic were actually involved in the cause of it, or that doctors might give irreversibly destructive drug treatments and surgeries to children and young adults with perfectly healthy bodies. For as long as these things remain unthinkable, or are bundled up and denounced as "right-wing talking points", people of medicine and science will continue to pursue mad but profitable projects, harming human health and putting our very survival at risk. They will be shielded by those of their own class, those in positions of power and in the media, who are inclined to trust them and support them, and who end up colluding with them and sharing in their guilt and denial. The collective culpability of their class is often in plain sight, but people do not want to look.

Things had changed, slowly, and then all at once, as they say. I had thought myself the good lefty, groaning in the 90s at people who complained about "political correctness" and disapproving of the sexist "lads mags" like *Loaded*; I had been something of an anti-sexist, anti-racist, right-on bore. But now I found myself under suspicion of being a right winger, and nearly everyone else was a lefty, which had become (in my humble or arrogant opinion) silly, controlling and (as bad as anything else) boring.

It was classic, contrary me, of course; if everyone is going one way I will be inclined to go another. Human culture is mimetic, and social media has proven to be a great consensus enforcer. To align with one's tribe, class or identity is a common sense survival instinct, but it is the form of common sense I likely lack the most. In my defence, conformity is the one form of common sense that can induce us to abandon all the others, getting us humans to do and think today what yesterday we would have thought diabolical or mad. It is unworldly and unwise to challenge what others more powerful have agreed upon, and those with status and a large stake in the game know to be more careful, but I was not one of those.

Enough. I am annoying you, I am sure. We will all believe what suits us, myself included. Dismiss my wild musings as the forgivable eccentricities of one over-excited contrarian, and stay with my little history to its end, for it is a tale of our times, whether you agree with my observations or not. I have given you abundant evidence of my foolishness in the past, to make it all the easier for you to laugh off my version of events in the present.

Blake said "If the fool would persist in his folly he would become wise." The question is, have I been persistent enough in my folly to achieve such enlightenment? Perhaps Blake was just wrong, and the persistent fool is the greater fool for it. This fool might have been wiser to speculate less.

*

I won an award, but I was not happy with it. (Goodness me, am I *never* agreeable?) The Americana Music Association UK wrote to me to ask me if I would accept the Grass Roots Award at their third annual award ceremony to take place at the Hackney Empire. The award, the email told me, "celebrates the sometimes unsung heroes of the UK Americana scene. It is presented to people working in the industry (in a capacity other than as artists) who have made outstanding efforts to support Americana music." I was to receive it in recognition for my efforts with Come Down & Meet The Folks.

So I was to be honoured as an unsung hero of UK Americana who had worked in a capacity other than as an artist? I was pretty galled by this; do I even have to explain why? Was that ungracious of me? Was it ignorance or just thoughtlessness on their part? It couldn't really be the former, they knew who I was, or, at least, some of them did. In the end I agreed to accept if it was awarded not to me personally, but to Come Down & Meet The Folks, with myself and Big Steve accepting the big night's non-musician award together. Sometimes I am too nice.

*

I didn't vote for Brexit, but I did have a bet on it. Placed a couple of months before the vote, it was the biggest sum I've ever risked. £400 at 6/4 won me £600 with my stake returned. I am not that keen on short odds betting, but I was sure enough of this one to think it a banker. If you give people an opportunity to vote against government, especially government in its most remote, unelected and inessential form, what do you expect people to do? I also had a smaller wager that David Cameron would resign after the vote. Cameron had vowed that he would remain as prime minister whatever the outcome, and as soon as I heard him say that, I knew what he would do if he lost.

So I wasn't that put out when the news came through that we had voted to leave the EU. Swings and roundabouts; my opinion was Brexit was fine in principle, messy in practice. I had no affection for the grey-suited men from Brussels who I had encountered working in the civil service. I had more sympathy with the old democratic socialists like Tony Benn, who preferred the kind of government you vote for directly, which can make all its own decisions. Another of this persuasion was my old north London party colleague Jeremy Corbyn, now the Labour leader, who had campaigned for decades to leave the EU, only to start going in the opposite direction when his desired objective came within reach. Mr Corbyn was soon being frogmarched by the party he was supposed to be leading towards a second referendum, to get the voters to have another go after they got the answer wrong the first time. If Corbyn had stuck to his guns and shown leadership and solidarity with Labour's old voters, many of whom were former miners who had battled Thatcher with him in the 80s, he might have realigned them with the modern left and become Prime Minister, but that was not going to happen, because his now middle class-dominated party considered Brexit-voting Labour voters too deplorable to have anything to do with.

If I thought the social media hate against Brexit supporters was bad before the vote, it was nothing to what came after, directed at the wicked white 'gammon', the great enemy within. Brexit was viewed as a hatred of foreigners by people who were great at spotting racism in others, but were hopeless at seeing how their own assumptions of cultural superiority played out in the world. I thought it was grim, especially when it came from my friends who had espoused a love for country music. I thought country music taught us that whites from humble origins had voices worth hearing just like the black folks did, that things were complicated and all communities deserve respect. That was the revelation of a song like *Okie From Muskogee* by Merle Haggard, a seminal record in our country music education. Merle had humorously given expression to pride in country, community and family and a shared suspicion of the "hippies out in San Francisco" who wanted to break down what they held dear. That the Okies had a story worth telling was a lesson I was not going to forget, but few of my contemporaries seemed to be remembering. When I pushed back on social media, questioning the progressive doctrines of open borders, free movement and gender identity, people reacted with incredulity: "What has happened to you?" I was asked.

What had happened to me? I was, of course, just me, carrying on being me. If I was alarmed at the present human condition and all its unreason, I was also fascinated with it, and tantalised by new insights and critical ideas. I anticipated a new essay by John Gray in the *New Statesman* or *Unherd* in much the same way as I used to look forward to the new single by Siouxsie and the Banshees.

It is true I had watched Jordan Peterson videos; perhaps that dark lord of disinformation had mesmerised me, exploiting my curiosity about Freud, Jung, Nietzsche and Dostoyevsky to lure me in. Peterson was full of interesting insights, I thought, but got cranky and tiresome as time went by, as a lot of these podcast people tend to do. Tickets for his talks at the O2 with Sam Harris were ridiculously expensive, which I baulked at, but that was true of all major performing artists, Peterson was not uniquely greedy. My main issue with him? I paid $20 to do his "self-authoring" personality test, and it gave me a low score on creativity. What absolute rubbish.

The idea that people like me think bad things because of the malign influence of newspapers and the internet is a view particularly popular with people who spend a lot of their time reading newspapers and going on the internet. Some will mock the less educated, but if you are more educated, might that not mean you are the more influenced? If you *were* brainwashed, you would hardly be aware of it. The power of the tabloid press is now absurdly overestimated by those who want to explain away the reasons people think what they do. I have had good record reviews in both the *Sun* and the *Mirror* in recent years, and I have discerned no positive influence on sales whatsoever. I jest.

Whatever. I was getting into trouble on social media: I was too opinionated to shut up when I saw things that infuriated me, but not thick-skinned enough to be able to take the flak that usually came for going against the grain. I wearied of that minute by minute state of low-level anxiety you get as you anticipate the reactions to your last killer comment, and compose yourself for your next riposte, which proves to be just as inconclusive as the last one. Some supported me when I kicked back against prevailing wisdoms, but the support was usually *sotto voce*. Others simply didn't mind or care, but I felt I was losing more than I was gaining, and, rightly or wrongly, I decided to cancel everyone before they cancelled me. I deleted my Facebook and Twitter accounts, and walked away from it all. It was another act of self-sabotage, I knew, but so be it. From then on, if I had something I wanted to say I would say it in person, or in song, or now, here.

*

The *Daily Telegraph* ran a Brexit poetry-writing competition. It was organised by Jacob Rees-Mogg's sister, I believe, but no matter. By the time I saw it, the competition had closed. All the entries could be viewed online. It was a motley collection: poems rhyming "Brexit" with "shit" were to the fore. I, of course, thought I could do better.

I had recently read David Goodhart's *The Road To Somewhere*. The book, with much supportive data, rethinks the nation's class divide as one between the Somewheres and the Anywheres. The Anywheres are the mobile, university-educated people who tend to manage things, and the Somewheres are more rooted in place and occupy roles that do not require higher education. The Anywheres have far more influence in society, have progressive/liberal politics, and our media and institutions tend to reflect back their preferences and prejudices. The Somewheres have little influence, and voted for Brexit in far greater numbers. The Anywheres blame the ill-educated Somewheres for our political woes, because they tend to say and think the wrong things and vote for all the wrong candidates. I'm inclined to blame the Anywheres for the state we are in, because they hold most of the power, and get their way most of the time, despite being frustrated at times by successive elected representatives. I am for the Somewheres, and I decided to write a poem for them: *Somewhere Better*.

Am I one of the Somewheres? Somewhat. I am part Somewhere and part Anywhere. I had a higher education, but I didn't travel far from home to get it. Most people I know are Anywheres, middle class people who had moved to London for education, jobs, or to be in bands; London-born lads I know like Dave Morgan (Leyton), BJ Cole (Enfield), Boz Boorer (Edgware), and James Walbourne (Muswell Hill) are exceptions, not the norm. A lack of mobility makes me more of a Somewhere: my parents held on to their terraced house in Middlesex, and in recent years, especially since the Covid lockdowns, I have been back there more often than not, to look out for them both. Much of this book has been written at the dining room table in the same front bay window where I typed my first fanzine on mum's Underwood.

Time was when people took pride in being of elevated stock, and to be of lowly origin was nothing to shout about. Those days are long gone, and we are now apt to play down our privileges and emphasise anything humble in our backgrounds. Both my mother and father's families, the Allens and the Tylers, had gone up a little in the world. The smoky old photographs we have of our Edwardian cockney ancestors from Clerkenwell and Walthamstow (Mum's grandfather Walter Powell, her mother Gladys, great-uncles Fred and Percy,

"Cousin Edie" and numerous unknowns) are succeeded in time by crisper images of Mum, family, guests and Nan's Pekinese dogs, lounging in the Allen's rather elegant front parlour in Cranmer Road, Edgware, a room I remember from my childhood, with the upright piano, walnut veneer television set and Capodimonte figurines. Dad's parents had prospered similarly. With a basic education, diligence and cheery good manners, Ted Tyler had made a good living as a life assurance agent for the Liverpool Victoria Friendly Society. The family had bought and lived in a succession of quite nice houses in and around Hendon, before retiring to a new bungalow in Worthing by the sea, where their son's young family would join them at weekends and for short holidays.

But despite this background of moderate advancement and advantage, my dear Dad still firmly identified as working class, and encouraged us all to think the same. Perhaps his struggle to continue our family's gentle upward progression, or prosper as impressively as his grammar school pals, had something to do with his outlook. Rebuffed by snooty people at a holiday guest house, he joked that the middle classes could see the invisible letters "WC" on our foreheads, and identified their own class by magically perceiving "MC" on the heads of their own kind. Our working class credentials had some validity according to Tony Benn's inclusive definition (if you worked for a wage you were working class), but reading George Orwell as a youth I learned we failed to qualify by that author's more exacting standard. If Dad had worked on the factory floor at Frigidaire instead of in accounts, and if we had rented one of the council houses on the other side of our garden fence, we would have been real WC people, but as an office worker on a monthly salary with a mortgage and a house of his own, Dad and the rest of us Tylers were lower middle class, and after school I moved among mainly MC people.

My poem became a song, and *Somewhere Better* is the first track on my last album, *Made In Middlesex,* most of which I recorded on location, as it were, with my OP-1 and computer. The song was intended to be something both Somewheres and Anywheres could relate to. In the end it made little impression on either side of the divide. If I thought my 'Brexit Pop' might attract some interest from a few readers of *Spiked,* I was soon to be disappointed. An announcement in the *Evening Standard* saying I was to play at a Brexit Creatives event in the Spread Eagle in Camden caused a small consternation among some people I knew, unbeknown to me at the time. That night I played *Somewhere Better* and a few of Blake's Songs Of Innocence, which seemed to go down well, but it failed to create a sufficient buzz of interest to prompt Farage and Co to ask me along to repeat the show at the Parliament Square Brexit Day celebration. It was a rejection that I experienced with some degree of relief.

I thought my song was a good one. I was pleased. It was a little preachy in tone, perhaps, but it said what I wanted to say; it testified. In trying to speak to the concerns and aspirations of others, I probably only ended up speaking for myself. Perhaps it represents my own wished-for world more than anyone else's. Perhaps, like a lot of country music, it expresses a yearning for a lost life or promise that can now only haunt us in the present.

Home for us should be a land
That's fit for winners, AND for losers.
Home for heroes AND for villains,
ALL us beggars can't be choosers.

All cannot be joined together,
Only closer, bring things near.
When we roar, or if we whisper,
Each should have a voice to hear.

Not for us some overreaching,
Brave new blinding future scheme.
You can keep your revolution;
Brick by brick we'll build our dream.

Know your dragon-slaying monsters
Poison our abundant land.
Plans to root out all the evils,
Serve to turn the soil to sand.

Oh we are England, we are Scotland,
We are not just Anywhere.
We are Wales and Northern Ireland,
London, Newry, Swansea, Ayr.

Glasgow, Neath, to Luton, Leicester,
Give your best and take a share.
We are here and all we want is,
Somewhere better, somewhere fair.

Somewhere greener, somewhere wiser,
Somewhere where we all can sing.
Somewhere you can earn a living,
Get a place and do your thing.

Somewhere's not a destination,
Somewhere is a settlement.
Yes, our nature is to nurture
And to care when days are spent.

*

When I eventually conquered my fear of Covid-19 sufficiently to leave the house after the first lockdown, I wandered the sparsely populated Kenton streets filming the passing pedestrians and scenes on my phone to make a video to go with one of my new songs, *Lucky People*. "*We don't do what we used to like, 'cos we don't like what we used to do,*" went the catchy chorus. It was liked a lot on Facebook (I was still on it then) but nothing else happened. The last song I wrote for the album was *Yesterday's Chips*, which along with a few other songs was recorded at Sean's with Rick Batey on bass and my former boating neighbour, Eddie Real on drums. The song recalled my final spat on social media.

> "*What has happened to you, my friend?*
> *Whatever happened to me?*
> *You used to be such a lovely bloke*
> *But seriously*
> *You're going out on a limb, my friend*
> *Going out on a wing*
> *And it's all, quite clearly*
> *NOT the done thing*"

It was a cancel culture cautionary tale, to be sure, leavened, so I hoped, with self-mockery at the old duffer in me who had failed to move with the times, but my antagonistic Facebook friend who had provided me with the first phrase of the song recognised his own words, and failed to see the joke. On Twitter he described the author of my song as a conspiracy theorist who had gone down a right-wing rabbit hole, and elsewhere on social media (so I was told) he disparaged my electronic music-making, which was a shame, because he had always liked my stuff before. It was all rather sad. He was sad, and I was sad. I was sad because a decent friend had turned on me, and he was sad because I had been abducted by aliens. Perhaps one day we will have a drink together again and laugh at ourselves.

*

What is truth? More than half a century has gone by since Johnny Cash, The Man In Black, went to the White House to sing a song by that name to US President Richard Nixon. Does the lonely voice of youth still cry out for truth, as his song declaimed ? None of the young have recently asked me for any guidance, but that is not surprising; I can't remember my young self seeking the wisdom of elders, way back when. If I were asked now, I would warn against trusting some all-knowing artificial intelligence portal. These contraptions might get most things right, but if you come to rely on them... wrong or right, how would you know?

I have reassured myself that a book like this is one thing an artificial intelligence could never write, relying as it does on private recollections beyond the domain of data in the public realm, but it is hardly free from low-level AI interference, with Google Docs correcting my grammar and spelling as I write. I have resisted for now all the other gizmos Google has encouraged me to adopt, but the temptation for writers to employ AI to improve their work by rewriting their last paragraph in the style of Tennessee Williams, for instance, may prove too tempting for even the highest integrity.

On consideration, I decided to invite AI to contribute something to my work. There may be a few of you who have read this far without having listened to any of my music. Am I any good, you may ask? I asked an artificial intelligence if I was a good songwriter, and this was its reply.

> *"Alan Tyler, best known as the frontman and songwriter for the British alternative country band The Rockingbirds, is generally considered a talented songwriter. The band was known for its blend of country and rock influences, and Alan Tyler's songwriting played a significant role in shaping their sound. While The Rockingbirds may not have achieved the same level of mainstream success as some other bands, they were well-regarded in the alternative country and indie music scenes. Alan Tyler's songwriting often received praise for its heartfelt and genuine*

storytelling, and his lyrics touched on themes like love, relationships, and everyday life, which are common subjects in country music. So, within the context of his genre, he is considered a good songwriter by many music enthusiasts."

So there you have it. A little equivocal but I really cannot complain. Take it with a pinch of salt, though, this website is far from reliable. It misinformed me that The Rockingbirds' Sean Read played guitar and pedal steel (he doesn't), and has worked with punk band Stiff Little Fingers (he never did). It also claims that *Come Down & Meet The Folks* was a 60s folk music show on British TV, presented by Ralph McTell, which is real parallel universe stuff.

*

The pursuit of truth can become an obsession like anything else; you just end up shouting at the television and freaking out your girlfriend, who will carry on thinking that Louis Theroux is a nice man, regardless of what you say. I try to be Zen, but then I forget. I have been praised for an honest approach to songwriting, and perhaps I've taken that a little to heart, and overdone it, to compensate for my want of other shining talents.

In times of fear and trembling some of us look to a higher power for truth and meaning, and in recent years I had been going to church. Formerly it was to take my elderly parents, but these days I go on my own, just for me. Perhaps when you have some kind of religious upbringing, to be drawn back in later life is quite likely. My disillusionment with politics has certainly urged this along. One of the downsides of Christianity is Christian rock, which is generally awful, but leaving aside that perhaps oxymoronic genre, it can be acknowledged that God still has many of the best tunes. Be warned, if I am to have a funeral, I do not want pop songs at it, just hymns. It is mean of me, I know, not only because most of my friends probably don't care to sing them, but also because the singing of hymns is not easy; they often come in unkind key signatures and present considerable breathing challenges, and, speaking for myself, I find they can be emotionally overwhelming, and make me choke up. If you want to know who is a good singer, give them a hymn to sing.

Does God provide the fixed point of certainty and authority from which all other truths can be derived? Some philosophers have thought so, or admit, like Nietzsche, that without God we are left anchorless and bereft. Our modern secular society does not seem to be happier, healthier or wiser than before. But though many can acknowledge we have lost something, few of us can bring ourselves to believe in God anymore. The problem is faith; even if you would like to believe, believing is hard, if not impossible.

For a while I thought I could just go along on a Sunday and do like the Christians do, and that would be enough. And you certainly can; you will likely be made welcome wherever you go, and find support and community generously given. But it is not good enough to go along just because you think it might do you some good, like some nourishing medicine to take, or a balm for the soul. To be a Christian you have to believe in the word of God and in Christ and his resurrection; that is what being a Christian is.

I joined a Christian dating website, and had this all explained to me on one of my dates. My meet-up had looked intriguing and promising; D was a musician whose mid-90s indie/Britpop band had shared one or two festival bills with The Rockingbirds, and we might have brushed shoulders at the Falcon, once upon a time. She had become successful and pretty famous, but had long ago given up her old life and possessions, and had devoted herself to Christ.

We had a long, long chat together, wandering around a park in Lewisham near where she had a room, sheltering under trees when it rained. It was a while after the first Covid lockdown in 2020. I tentatively advanced my theory that living as a Christian, and doing as the Christians did, was the best I could do. My companion was not impressed. She thought I had to do better, a lot better. I was a little crestfallen, because I was there to impress, and had arrived with hopes of doing well with this enigmatic and still attractive former rock star.

D spoke of religious experiences, far more profound and powerful than the acid trips of her rock'n'roll youth, that had done much to confirm her in her faith. She asked if there had been any such experiences in my life. I admitted there had not. I might also have admitted that I had never wanted any. Part of my induction as a Roman Catholic at St Bernadette's Primary School was the story of our school saint's vision of the Virgin at the grotto in Lourdes. As an over-imaginative child the tale spooked and disturbed me, and sometimes when alone at night I would terrify myself by imagining the Virgin was about to appear to me just as she had to poor Bernadette.

So religious experiences were not for me, and I was not for D. She told me I was "on a journey" and so we departed, not to meet again. But since then, I think I have had a religious experience, and it was one that was not at all frightening, or even terribly weird. I only ever told one person about it, as I will shortly explain, but I thought I would put it down here for all to read, to end my story.

*

It was December 2022, and I was on the tube to Oxford Circus to do some Christmas shopping. I wanted to go to Liberty to get a few fancy things for my near and dear. I was sitting in a typical tube-train carriage, where the seats are all in a line along one side, facing the same the other. Most of the seats were occupied, and I was enjoying, as I often do, a guilt-free gaze at the random selection of fellow earthlings sitting opposite me, in all their funny familiarity and mystery.

Not right opposite me, but two or three seats to my right, I noticed a woman was looking at me, and she started to smile. Was she really smiling at me? I have smiled back before at someone who is smiling at someone else, so I am cautious, but a quick glance about me told me no, not this time; her smile was for me; she was looking straight at me.

She was perhaps a little older than I, quite slight, wearing glasses, a greying untidy bob of hair, ill-fitting jeans and a little anorak; perhaps not English, perhaps a solitary traveller abroad. She saw I had caught her eye, and she smiled more warmly. I smiled back, very tentatively, and my mind began to race. Do I know this woman? I wondered. Often people recognise me and expect me to know them, but I am bad at recalling old acquaintances and worry that I will offend by not remembering. I scoured the index of my memory, but nothing registered. No, I thought, I am *sure* I do not know who this woman is. She did not look like anyone I might have known. Not a music person, I thought to myself, someone I'd know that way. I looked over at her again, and this time she gave me the warmest smile, a really big, sustained and open smile, that hit me directly with a wave of love. Oh my God, I thought. Oh. My. God! And no, she was *not* coming on to me. No. Not at all. I smiled back at her with greater confidence, but then it got too much and I looked away again, a little embarrassed, not knowing quite what to do. Shortly after, the train drew into the next station, and she got up to go. Our eyes met with one last glimpse of acknowledgement, and then she was gone.

I was left trying to make sense of what had happened. I wished that I had at least said "Merry Christmas" as she left. That would have been nice of me, to reciprocate a little more of what she had just sent my way. Tears welled up in my eyes and threatened to embarrass me on the train. It was love, that was all. Love just for the sake of love. Love that said, "Have some love from me, for free". Love from out of nowhere. Love out of nothing. Love that said, "You are alright, you are OK, you are good, you are loved and you are not alone, or forgotten, and you never will be." It was love that came from God, I was sure. I was as sure she had come to me from God as I was of anything I have ever been sure of in my life. What more did I want? What more could I want?

We humans love angels, do we not? We sing and write songs about them and tell tales of them in some of our favourite movies and stories. Angels bring divinity into our lives. I have not seen my Angel Lady since that day, but I try to think of her often, as a friend I can call to mind for help and encouragement. What would my Angel Lady like me to do? Would she like to see me doing this? I sometimes ask myself things like that. I am told in church to look to the Virgin for such guidance, and I do, but my Angel Lady has somehow made that all the easier, so I hope it is OK for me to hold onto my heavenly friend, just for the time being. Do angels really exist? Don't be ridiculous. Did I really see an angel? Of course I did.

Leaving Oxford Circus Station, before going about my Christmas shopping, I went looking for the nearest church, to reflect and say a little "thank you", and found the Welsh Church in Eastcastle Street. A man with a big beard was at the door, the organist, just opening up to do some practising or whatever else he planned to do that day. He let me in and was keen to chat. He assumed I was wanting to admire the church's interesting features more than wanting to pray. I indulged him and told him about my church, St Andrews in Kingsbury, explaining it had been moved, stone by stone and brick by brick, from its former location in nearby Mortimer Street to its present location 85 years ago. The organist corrected me: it was moved from Wells Street, not Mortimer Street. He knew all about St Andrews, and our fine organ, which is now in need of some costly repair.

I really wanted to have a little word with The Man Above, rather than chat about church organs, but after a few quiet moments of that, I ventured to break the silence to tell him about my heavenly encounter on the train. He listened, I think, but after I had finished my short account, he left a moment's pause and then began talking about something else. Oh well, I thought, this nice man has let me into his church assuming I am an ordinary sightseer, and now he fears he may have a mad stranger on his hands, who claims visions of angels. I thought it kindest to relieve him of any such worries, and asked him to show me the way out; I had some shopping to do.

*

What now for me? Perhaps I should take further inspiration from the great hillbilly bard Hank Williams, and pen a few tunes to give thanks and praise to the Lord. Maybe. I cannot be sure how much further my musician friends will be willing to accompany me on such flights, but "further up and further in"... we shall see. As a matter of fact, I wrote a Christmas carol a couple of years ago, but our church organist wasn't that impressed, and wanted the music written out before he would trouble himself to play it. Maybe I can get Sean on to that. I need to up my game.

At the end of *Down And Out In Paris And London* George Orwell leaves a pithy list of things he had learned on his vagabond adventures: never give money to the Sally Army, always accept handbills, don't eat tripe, things like that. My aim was to explain how to never have a hit. For those who want to do better than I have done, here is a summary of my lessons learnt.

1. Don't try to be different, go with the flow. Be like the rest, only more so.
2. Don't join the Cult Of The Can't; it is OK to start out not knowing how, but do not resolve to remain that way.
3. Make sure you use modern and industry-standard recording equipment that works properly.
4. Be chatty and friendly, and make lots of friends. If you are going to say something mean, at least don't put it in writing.
5. Believe in magic, but don't *only* believe in magic. Music can be a nice job, but it is still a job, and the only way to get the magic to work is to work.

6. Don't break up your band once they have made a name for themselves; keep the name going, come what may. Multiple entities only muddle your message.
7. Avoid tap dancing on hard stone floors.

I still hope for an improvement in my musical fortunes. A successful book may help nudge up my monthly Spotify interest from the hundreds to the thousands, and then ascend to some even greater figure. Imagine! Yes, that is the plan, the great and perhaps final plan. But if my literary effort, this last gambit, proves to be all in vain (and all is vanity, after all)... well then, such is my destiny. For plans coming to not a fat lot are my stock in trade, as this book should now have adequately demonstrated.

Adored or ignored are just things you can be. *"Amor fati"* was the advice given by that great 19th century self-help guru Friedrich Nietzsche. I am with him on that, if nothing else. And so I am determined to embrace my fate, to say a little prayer, and to die happy.

Adieu!

Discography

A list of the main record releases by The Rockingbirds and Alan Tyler

Albums
The Rockingbirds (1992) Heavenly/Columbia HVNLP 2
Whatever Happened To The Rockingbirds (1995) Heavenly/Cooking Vinyl COOK 084
Faithful by Alan Tyler (2002) Littlefield Records LITTLECD001
Alan Tyler & The Lost Sons Of Littlefield (2006) Hanky Panky Records HPR006
So Far by Alan Tyler (2007) Hanky Panky Records HPR010
Lonesome Cowboys by Alan Tyler & The Lost Sons Of Littlefield (2008) Hanky Panky Records HPR011
The Return Of The Rockingbirds (2013) Loose VJCD205
The Alan Tyler Show (2015) Littlefield LIT002
William Blake's Songs Of Innocence (2015) YouTube video release
El Tapado by Alan Tyler (2018) Hanky Panky Records HPR034
More Rockingbirds (2019) Hanky Panky Records HPR041
Made In Middlesex by Alan Tyler (2021) Hanky Panky Records HPR057

Singles and EPs
By The Rockingbirds
Your Good Girl's Gonna Go Bad/Lovesick Blues (1991) Clawfist 7" XPIG 9
A Good Day For You Is A Good Day For Me/Jonathan Jonathan/Only One Flower (1991) Heavenly HVN14
Jonathan Jonathan b/w *Time Drives The Truck/The Older Guys* (1992) Heavenly//Columbia HVN 17

Gradually Learning b/w *Where I Belong/Love Has Gone And Made A Mess Of Me* (1992) Heavenly/Columbia HVN 21
Rockingbirds "R" Us EP (1993) Heavenly HVN 31
Band Of Dreams b/w *Everybody Lives With Us* (1994) Heavenly 7" HVN 43
Man In The Moon b/w *Lookingback Lullaby* (2009) Heavenly 7" HVN 190
Till Something Better Comes Along b/w *Fixing The Roof In Your Dream* (2011) 7" Spring Records Spring4

By Famous Times
Springboard/Something To Believe 7" (1997) Label: Heavenly HVN 62
The Blue Man EP 10"/CD (1997) Label: Heavenly HVN 69

Picture information

Photos taken or owned by Alan Tyler unless stated.

Page 13 – Photo from Bakerloo line train carriage (2024)
Page 22 – Family photographs, Joe Allen in the foreground.
Page 36 – Front cover of *Cool* fanzine #1 (1979)
Page 42 – Street Level Studio ad. Origin/ownership not known (c. 1980)
Page 53 – Igor, Dave Morgan, Alan Tyler (c. 1980/81)
Page 58 – Take It outside the Rock Garden in Covent Garden. Left to right: Barbara Snow, Igor, Jim Wannell, Etta Saunders, Dave Morgan, Alan Tyler. Photo by Coneyl Jay (c. 1982/83)
Page 86 – The prehistoric Rockingbirds. Left to right: Stan Patrzalek, Alan Tyler, Phoebe Flint. Photo by Paul White (c. 1988/89)
Page 87 – The Weather Prophets. Left to right: Pete Astor, Piece Thompson, Dave Morgan, Dave "Greenwood" Goulding. Photo by Rob White (c. 1988)
Page 99 – The Rockingbirds. Alan Tyler with guitar, and clockwise from left: Dave Goulding, Patrick Arbuthnot, Sean Read, Andy Hackett, Dave Morgan, Elliot the dog. Photo by Robin Brookes. (c. 1990/91)
Page 102 – The Rockingbirds outside 123 Camden Road. Clockwise from bottom left: Sean Read, Patrick Arbuthnot, Dave Morgan, Dave Goulding, Andy Hackett, Alan Tyler. Photo by Ski Williams (1991)
Page 103 – Flyer for the Rockingbirds Rolling Revue at the Borderline, London (c. 1991)
Page 111 – Jonathan Richman (foreground) with The Rockingbirds, taken backstage at the Mean Fiddler, London. Photo by Duncan Brown (1991)
Page 119 – Rockingbirds recording session at Westside Studios. At the recording desk (left to right): Danton Supple (engineer), Chris Potter (engineer) and Clive Langer (producer). Behind (left to right): Strobe, Martin Kelly, Jeff & Wendy Barrett, Dave Morgan, Alan Tyler. Photo by Paul Kelly (1992)
Page 120 – Photo machine picture of the gang in Austin, Texas, making the *Gradually Learning* video. Clockwise from bottom right: Andy Hackett, Dave Morgan, Sean Read, Alan Tyler, Tony Van Den Ende (director), Cathy Hood (producer), Patrick Arbuthnot and Jeff Barrett (1992)

Page 124 – *The Rockingbirds* album cover. Designed by Ski Williams (1992)
Page 130 – Alan Tyler on *Later With Jools Holland (1992)*.
Page 134 – The Rockingbirds with racehorse Road To Riches. Photo by Steve Gullick (1992)
Page 138 – The Rockingbirds belt buckle (2024)
Page 140 – Jackie Hendrie and Anna Tyler-Ahmed at Blow Up (c.1996)
Page 159 – Polaroid of Alan Tyler in The Engine Room, Camden, taken by Jimmy Smith of the Gourds (c. 1997)
Page 163 – Big Steve and Alan Tyler hosting Come Down & Meet The Folks at The Golden Lion, Camden. Photographer unknown (c. 2002)
Page 165 – T-shirt design by Ski Williams (c. 2003)
Page 167 – *Time Out* album review (2002)
Page 169 – Edward The Troubadour at Rosie O'Grady's. Photographer unknown (c. 2000)
Page 173 – Alan Tyler & The Lost Sons Of Littlefield. Photo by Alenka Banic (c. 2006)
Page 174 – Tapestry Goes West poster. Design by Nervous Stephen (2002)
Page 175 – Sheriff JB in Silver City, Cornwall (2002)
Page 176 – Barry Stillwell and some horses at the Spirit Of The West theme park, Cornwall (2002)
Page 183 – Hackney Empire dressing room door (2007)
Page 190 – Andy Hackett at The Scala. Photo by Ruth Tidmarsh (c. 2011)
Page 194 – The Rockingbirds outside the Grand Ole Opry, Glasgow. Left to right: Patrick Ralla, Mark Duncan, Patrick Arbuthnot, Dave Morgan, Andy Hackett, Alan Tyler. Photo by John Brandham (2013)
Page 200 – The Come Down & Meet The Folks backdrop, designed by Alison Vickers (2004)
Page 204 – Selfie on Deptford Creek (c. 2015)
Page 206 – Birds Nest toilet. Photo by Dave McGowan (c. 2015)
Page 216 – Teenage Engineering OP-1 synthesiser
Page 218 – El Tapado (c. 2018)
Page 228 – Walter Powell (family photo)
Page 229 – Christina Tyler (née Allen) and Dennis Tyler (family photo)
Page 247 – Andy Hackett and Sean Read at Cambridge Folk Festival. Photo by Chris Clarke (1992).

Acknowledgements

I am grateful to all who have helped me in different ways in the course of producing this book. Without their support I would have given up long ago.

The greatest thanks go to Rick Batey, my earliest confidante, who has been a consistent source of suggestions, encouragement and all-round writerly advice, and to my old friend Becky Stewart, who helped me to put the design together. Thanks also, of course, to John Niven, not just for the foreword but for the observations and thoughtful criticisms he offered last year.

Thanks are also variously due, for great helps and for small ones, to: Paul Burke (my Kenton contemporary), Shaun Hendry (Bucks Music), Paul Beveridge (aka Beaver the Postman), Jeff Barrett, James Strobe Scott, Ken Copsey, Maddy Clarke, Marc Mikulich, Steve "Igor" Wright, Caroline Catz, Barry Stillwell, Antony Harwood, Mark Duncan, Iñaki Orbezua, Ski Williams, Richard "Raz" Cobbings, Anna Tyler-Ahmed, Patrick Ralla, Chris Clarke, Andy Hackett, Sean Read and all the people mentioned at the front (Sukie, Pete, Andrew M, David Q and John M) who read *How To Never Have A Hit* and said good things about it.

Thank you to all my other friends, and, most of all, thank you to my wonderful, supportive and loving family.

I am very much obliged to you all.

Alan Tyler - October 2024

Cheers!